THE MIDDLE GRADE TEACHER'S
HANDBOOK
FOR
COOPERATIVE
LEARNING

by Terri Breeden and Janice Mosley

Incentive Publications, Inc.
Nashville, Tennessee

Cover design by Susan Eaddy

ISBN 0-86530-224-3

TABLE OF CONTENTS

ABOUT THIS BOOK

In order to survive in the work force, people must exhibit cooperative behaviors. This book is designed to help teachers implement cooperative learning in the classroom.

The first portion is a simple handbook on the teaching method of cooperative learning and how it can be implemented easily in any classroom. The second portion contains actual lesson plans designed for the middle school teacher. Lessons include math, language arts, science, and social studies. There is also a unit of seven lessons dealing with problem-solving.

Designed with the busy middle school teacher in mind, this source contains 32 lesson plans and numerous supplemental materials. These innovative cooperative lessons include the following components:

- Cooperative lesson plans
- Ideas for using the textbook
- Role-playing activities
- Cooperative learning work sheets
- Group processing activities
- Helpful hints
- Individual follow-up activities
- Enrichment activities
- Games

Suggestions for the use of these lessons are numerous. They can be used in a specific subject area, for exploratory classes, or in a teacher/advisor period. Many of the lessons can be adapted easily for remediation or enrichment-type activities in the middle school.

As you implement cooperative learning, the rewards of a cooperative classroom should soon be apparent among the students.

WHAT IS COOPERATIVE LEARNING?

DEFINITION OF COOPERATIVE LEARNING

Cooperative learning is students working together in structured groups helping each other learn and earning rewards for their efforts.

"Students working together" – The classroom teacher divides the class into small groups. These groups should have between two and six members. They should consist of high, medium, and low achieving students.

"Helping each other learn" – The students are assigned a specific task. Then, the groups help one another do the assignment. When the assignment is done, each student should have acquired the knowledge or skills necessary to do a similar assignment on his/her own, without the help of others.

"Earning rewards" – A positive reinforcement point system is used to reward groups that follow cooperative norms of behavior and demonstrate the ability to master skills practiced in the cooperative groups.

WHERE DOES COOPERATIVE LEARNING FIT INTO CURRENT TEACHING METHODS?

Now that you know what cooperative learning is, how does it fit in with the other teaching methods currently in use? There are seven basic teaching methods in use in today's classroom. Cooperative learning should not replace these methods, rather it should be used in lessons that lend themselves to a group cooperative effort. The teaching methods used in the classroom are the following:

- **Individual Task Structure** - The students study the same work individually.
- **Small Group Task Structure** - This is the category where cooperative learning is found.
- **Tutorial Structure** - The teacher reteaches individual students.
- **Didactic Structure** - The teacher lectures to the students.
- **Conference Structure** - The teacher asks a question and then allows the students to solve the problems.
- **Class Meeting Structure** - This is the same setup as the conference structure except the teacher is involved in the problem-solving.
- **Socratic Method** - The teacher answers a question with a question (Shearer, 1990).

WHAT IS COOPERATIVE LEARNING?

COOPERATIVE LEARNING BEGINS WITH COOPERATIVE TEACHING

Learning something new or changing the way something has been done is a painful and difficult process. Beginning to use cooperative learning techniques in the classroom is no different. There will be days when everything about cooperative learning clicks and the students achieve more than one had hoped. However, there will also be days when nothing seems right. The best way to get through the disappointing days is to have a teaching partner — someone who is using cooperative learning techniques and would be willing to go over a lesson and brainstorm to improve it. Even if all the lessons and activities are going well, a partner is someone with whom to share the success.

THINGS TO REMEMBER

☞ **Move slowly into cooperative learning.**

In a self-contained classroom, begin in only one subject area, then expand. If teaching is done in a departmentalized setting, begin with only one class and then implement in other classes.

☞ **Stick with it!**

In a two-day activity, the second day is usually the best. The class understands the assignment and has adjusted to the cooperative group.

☞ **Plan the cooperative activity carefully.**

Planning cannot be emphasized enough. The activity must be organized so that students have to cooperate in order to successfully complete the activity.

☞ **Use existing materials and text.**

Sometimes new cooperative lessons are desired, but most of the time a simple adjustment in a textbook page is all that is necessary. (See the BLUEPRINT pages for general suggestions [pages 30, 51, 52, 69, and 86].)

WHAT IS COOPERATIVE LEARNING?

HOW TO CHOOSE A CRITERION FOR COOPERATIVE LEARNING GROUPS

In order to organize the cooperative groups, some type of base score should be used. Base scores could be derived from a pretest, report card grade, last year's average in a particular subject, an achievement test score, teacher judgment, or a combination of scores. After a score is selected, follow the organizational sheets on pages 12 through 14.

THINGS TO CONSIDER WHEN FORMING GROUPS

How many members should be in each group? Research states that cooperative groups should consist of two to six members. Literature also supports that at first it is best to begin with small groups. Students will need to practice working cooperatively, and smaller groups seem to allow the students more opportunities to practice cooperative skills.

The nature of the cooperative activities themselves affects the determination of group size. If a group is proofreading for one another, perhaps a group of two is the most appropriate. Yet a larger group is great if a research project is assigned.

To be very practical, a teacher needs to look at the materials and space he/she has available when determining group size. If an activity requires geoboards, the number of geoboards available will affect the number of cooperative groups established. If an activity requires tables and the classroom has only six tables, then six groups is the maximum one can have.

Attendance can be a major factor in the size of cooperative groups. It would be unwise to have groups of two if the class has a high rate of absenteeism. The teacher would be reorganizing groups constantly when students are absent.

The roles of the students may determine the size of the groups. If there are numerous tasks, a larger group would be appropriate.

WHAT IS COOPERATIVE LEARNING?

OTHER THINGS TO CONSIDER

Grouping students who would not normally seek out each other's company is a great way to begin friendships and have good cooperative groups. Examine the ethnic makeup of the class. Organize cooperative groups with a good blend of males and females. Cross ethnic lines and socio-economic levels. Be prepared for students to initially voice their displeasure in group assignments. If initially the teacher has already done some interpersonal activities with the class, the best solution to displeasure is to ignore it. Most of the time, the students are just upset that they are not with their best friends. Be prepared to visit each group and praise the students for following cooperative norms of behavior. As the students begin to work together, they begin to see the strengths of each group member. If after several cooperative activities there is still an interpersonal problem, then do intervene at that point.

WHAT ABOUT MAINSTREAMING?

Mainstreaming and cooperative learning go hand-in-hand. Cooperative activities provide an opportunity for handicapped students and regular education students to work side by side. A cooperative classroom provides a great environment for the mainstreamed child. One real advantage of using cooperative learning with the mainstreamed child is the effect it has on self-esteem.

Some preparation is necessary to integrate the mainstreamed child into the classroom. Suggested activities include providing a similar assignment to the child's resource teacher the day before the cooperative activity. It is possible that the handicapped child could become an expert on the lesson. Another suggestion is to pair the handicapped student with a high achieving student before the cooperative activity. The two students would review the assignment before meeting with the entire cooperative group.

When the mainstreamed child is in the group, demonstrate specific techniques that will ensure the handicapped student is truly understanding the work. A useful technique is to ask the handicapped student to state how an answer was derived rather than simply listening to students give explanations.

A final suggestion to help the mainstreamed child is to structure the materials or the roles in the group so that the handicapped student is involved. The mainstreamed child could have the role of getting the supplies from the table or he/she could be the encourager for the group. These simple roles would ensure that the student was included in some fashion.

ORGANIZING COOPERATIVE GROUPS

Step 1 - List the students in your class. Place the student with the highest base score first. Continue to list the students in "top-down" order. The student with the lowest base score should be the last student on the list.

Step 2 - On the first chart, fill in the base scores, sex, race, and any other information that would help you when organizing cooperative groups. (See page 14.)

Step 3 - Decide how many groups you want and how many students in each group.

Step 4 - Select your first group by choosing the student with the top base score. Place a "1" by his/her name under the section "Group Number." Then select the student with the lowest base score. Place "1" by his/her name. Fill in the rest of the group with students with middle range base scores. If you are forming groups of three, select one student with a middle base score. If you desire groups of four, select two middle range students. Continue until the first group is selected. Now select the other groups following this same pattern. Continue until all students have been assigned a group number.

ORGANIZING COOPERATIVE GROUPS

Step 5 - Look over your groups. Are they satisfactory?
Do you have a good balance of boys and girls?
Are they racially and ethnically balanced? Did
you put discipline problems in the same group?
How about the mainstreamed child? How does
his/her group look? In general, do you see any
reason to do some shifting? If so, shift students
who have similar abilities.

Step 6 - List the groups below. Fill in each student's
base score.

Group 1

_____

_____

_____

Group 2

_____

_____

_____

Group 3

_____

_____

_____

Group 4

_____

_____

_____

Student Name	Base Score	Group Number	Sex	Race	Other

PLANNING THE ACTUAL COOPERATIVE ACTIVITY

SPACE/ROOM ARRANGEMENT

If the classroom has a traditional arrangement, thirty student desks and one teacher's desk, the best bet would be to assign students to seats so groups are already sitting near each other. In a noncooperative activity, the desks remain in rows or in whatever arrangement is preferred. When it is time for cooperative groups to form, the students can easily move the desks so they are in a group facing each other.

MATERIALS

Be sure enough materials are available and that they are easily accessible. Have a plan for distributing supplies. Have the materials in a central location.

WRITTEN INSTRUCTIONS

Instructions need to be clear and easily understood. They should be written so that the students must cooperate to solve the activity rather than in a way that allows students to work independently. Writing effective instructions takes practice. It is helpful to ask a fellow teacher to review the directions or work sheet before it is given to the cooperative group.

GROUP PROCESSING SKILLS

Students have been taught repeatedly to keep their eyes on their own paper, not to share homework, and to be responsible for their own grades. Due to this previous training, cooperative skills must be taught. Many teachers do not see the importance of teaching these skills, yet cooperative skills are essential in marriage, jobs, and future friendships. It has been reported that 10 percent of school-age children have no friends! The Center of Public Resources in the U.S. Work Force found that about 90 percent of the respondents who were fired from their jobs were fired for poor job attitude, poor interpersonal relationships, and inappropriate behavior. Being fired for lack of technical skill was infrequent (Johnson and Johnson, 1989).

PLANNING THE ACTUAL COOPERATIVE ACTIVITY

What exactly are these "cooperative skills," and how can they be taught? A general listing of cooperative skills follows:

- expressing support
- listening
- summarizing
- contributing ideas
- expressing feelings
- checking for understanding
- using quiet voices
- moving quietly to the group

- giving directions to the group
- encouraging participation
- explaining answers
- accepting other right answers
- relating past learning to present
- criticizing ideas, not people
- asking probing questions
- requesting further rationale

In order to have successful, interdependent, cooperative groups, teachers need to directly teach these skills to students. First, the teacher must impress upon students the value of the skill. This task can be accomplished through class discussion or role play. A bulletin board emphasizing the need for any of the skills would also be a good technique. When the students demonstrate any of the cooperative skills in the classroom, the teacher could praise the behavior and point out how that behavior is very appropriate in a cooperative group setting.

Johnson and Johnson (1990) have developed a very useful technique called the T-Chart (see illustration). The skill to be mastered is written at the top of the T. On one side of the T the students list what the skill would look like, and on the other side of the T the students list what the skill would sound like.

Explaining Answers

Looks Like:	Sounds Like:
1.	1.
2.	2.
3.	3.

PLANNING THE ACTUAL COOPERATIVE ACTIVITY

When teaching cooperative skills, one need not prepare long detailed lessons. A good plan of action would be to isolate a particular cooperative skill and spend a few minutes explaining and demonstrating it. The class could then be told that today **that** is the skill of emphasis. The teacher could verbally praise the student when the skill is demonstrated. The teacher may also want to tell the class that a tally will be taken on the number of times that skill is demonstrated. If that skill is demonstrated a certain number of times, a reward will be given. It's hard to teach cooperative skills to children who have been in an individualistic or competitive classroom. At first, students will feel a little silly or fake with these new skills, but continue to encourage them until it becomes part of their repertoire.

COOPERATIVE NORMS OF BEHAVIOR

When a teacher hears about children moving their desks and sitting together in groups, the thought of classroom chaos comes to mind. This can be the case if the class loses its structure during the cooperative learning activity. It would be wise for the classroom teacher to post specific cooperative group rules. Each teacher must come up with a set of rules that fits his/her particular behavioral expectations. Before the first cooperative activity is done, the teacher should envision what a productive, orderly, cooperative classroom would look like and then write rules that will lead to this vision.

One of the most effective discipline techniques to use in a classroom is the teacher's proximity to the students. The teacher should be monitoring the classroom during the activity. If a group is off task, stand by one of the group members. This is usually an effective method for getting the activity back on track. If the class is misbehaving, then begin rewarding and praising students that are following norms of behavior. It is amazing how effective this simple technique is. If misconduct still occurs, deal with it in the normal fashion. Chaos does not belong in a cooperative classroom.

PLANNING FOR INTERDEPENDENCE

Interdependence is a key word in cooperative learning. It denotes the art of students in a group realizing that it takes all members to achieve a goal. Proponents of cooperative learning suggest that posting slogans in the classroom is one simple method for creating an atmosphere of interdependence. Johnson and Johnson suggest the phrase, "Sink or Swim - we are all in this together."

PLANNING THE ACTUAL COOPERATIVE ACTIVITY

Lesson plans must be organized to facilitate group work, but interdependence goes beyond an assignment with four students' names on the top of the paper. The group must feel that all members must be successful in order for the group to be successful.

Planning the cooperative activity for interdependence is essential. The first step is assigning specific roles to each group member and then monitoring the classroom to see that the group members are playing their roles. (See THE STUDENT'S ROLE, page 19.) It is also imperative that each student understand that he/she is responsible for learning the material and making sure that all other group members learn the assigned material and complete the assignment.

CLASSWIDE INTERDEPENDENCE

A teacher must be aware that to keep a classwide feeling of cooperation, he/she must plan for a feeling of total class success. If this aspect of planning is not included, a strong group competitive atmosphere could evolve. Some competition between groups is acceptable, but the total class feeling of interdependence is best.

Ways that class interdependence could be fostered are numerous. An easy method for implementation could be a class reward when a set number of improvement points are achieved in the class. Free homework passes could be handed out if no one in the class fails a test. The lesson plan, "Cooperative Soup," page 41, is an example of how a teacher can plan for classwide interdependence. Each group must interdependently do its part of the lesson in order to help create the finished product for the class. Without a contribution from each group, there is no finished product.

COOPERATIVE GROUP ROLES

THE STUDENT'S ROLE

Students will be more likely to work together cooperatively if they have been assigned specific group roles and if they know the responsibilities required for each role. It seems that more success is achieved if the student roles remain constant for a set number of weeks. This longer assignment of roles seems to give the students time to fully understand all aspects of the job. The specific roles are as follows:

- ❑ **Runner** - This is the only person in the group allowed to ask the teacher to assist the group. He/she asks for assistance only if no one else in the group can solve the problem.
- ❑ **Checker** - The checker has two responsibilities. First, he/she double-checks all answers on individual papers as well as the **one** paper the group will turn in for a grade. The checker is also responsible for making sure everyone knows and can explain the answers.
- ❑ **Reporter** - The reporter records the group's answers on a work sheet to submit for a group grade.
- ❑ **Encourager** - The encourager encourages full participation by asking all members to offer their opinions, views, or answers.

If there are more than four members in the group, other roles can be used, such as reader, praiser, summarizer, timekeeper, materials manager, and sergeant at arms. Be sure to explain each role's responsibilities and check to be sure the students are performing these responsibilities.

THE TEACHER'S ROLE

The teacher has already been busy organizing cooperative groups, assigning student roles, and planning the actual cooperative activity. At this point, students are ready to begin working. Whew! Now the teacher can sit down and rest, right? Wrong! This is where the teacher really begins to work. The teacher will monitor the groups and intervene when necessary to assure the students are working cooperatively and successfully.

COOPERATIVE GROUP ROLES

The teacher's role is essential to success. The roles of the teacher are numerous. They include the following:

☞ **Observer -** The teacher should use some type of formal observation sheet to mark how often he/she observes appropriate behaviors. Do not try to check for all appropriate behaviors at one time; just watch for a few behaviors during each activity. Let the students know which behaviors are being observed. The hope is that the students will attempt to model them for the teacher.

☞ **Resource Person -** Teachers should be sure they give cooperative groups the time to solve problems that arise rather than jumping in to assist them at the first sign of trouble. However, if a group is genuinely unable to continue, the teacher needs to work with the group. Do not forget that the teacher should truly be helping the **group** rather than **individual** members of the group.

☞ **Troubleshooter -** Sometimes groups will have problems with cooperative skills that make it impossible for them to successfully complete the work. Typical group problems include the following:

- Students are not listening to each other.
- Students do not stay on task.
- Not all the students are participating equally.
- Teammates are not helping each other.
- Teammates are not praising and encouraging each other.
- Students are talking too loudly.
- Students are not completing their responsibilities (Kagan, 1989).

There are four approaches that can be taken to solve these problems:

First, reinforce positive behavior by verbally praising the teams that are successfully modeling these cooperative skills.

Second, assign roles to the students. Make certain the roles are clearly defined and understood before an assignment is given.

Third, the teacher should have a group processing paper for the team to fill out at the end of the activity. This is when students answer questions about the use of social skills on the day's assignments. Possible questions could be: 1) Did I use a quiet voice? 2) Did I stay on task? 3) Did I ask for help when I needed it? 4) Did I give help when others needed it?

Fourth, the teacher builds structure into the actual cooperative activity that leads to developing these social skills. Methods used in dealing with common problems are suggested on page 21.

COOPERATIVE GROUP ROLES

Problem	Possible Solutions
Not listening	Before a student can offer an idea, he/she must tell what the last person said.
Not staying on task	Teacher assigns bonus points to any team that has every member staying on task.
Unequal participation	Assign each group member an equal number of chips or strips of paper. Whenever a member of the team contributes an idea, he/she places a chip in the center of the table. When a student runs out of chips, he/she may not contribute again until everyone is out of chips. Then they are redistributed and the members start all over again.
Not praising each other	In order to share an idea, the student must find something positive to praise about the previous speaker.
Talking too loudly	The teacher rewards the entire class if they can go a set amount of time using quiet voices.
Failing to complete	When each member of the team finishes his/her assignments, the group receives a reward. One possible reward might be to receive bonus points.
General misconduct	When general misconduct occurs, the teacher should discipline in accordance with the set classroom rules.

STUDENT AND GROUP ACCOUNTABILITY

STUDENT ACCOUNTABILITY

Someone once said, "Folks tend to do better when they know they are being watched!" Cooperative groups must be watched carefully to ensure everyone is accountable. The teacher can use several methods and techniques to make certain that no "freeloaders" are found in the cooperative classroom. One useful technique is questioning. The teacher simply questions individual students or groups about the assignment as he/she monitors the classroom.

If a teacher needs a formal assessment, he/she can assign an individual work sheet or test on the skills the students should have learned cooperatively. Since the students will now be working individually, they do not ask each other for help. The grade they receive on this paper counts for them individually, and it will be used to assign the team points. (See grade point system on page 23.)

When the teams are working on the same assignment but each student completes a separate answer sheet, the teacher can randomly select one paper from the group. The grade on this paper is the grade each team member receives. It is very important for students to check each other's work and agree on the final answers on every paper since they do not know which paper will be chosen.

Another easy way to assess individual accountability is the use of student demonstrations and explanations. At the end of class, students share reports on how to work a problem on the chalkboard or overhead projector. Science, home economics, art, and physical education lend themselves well to student demonstrations.

Occasionally the teacher needs to give an observation sheet to one member of each team. That member refrains from participating in the day's activities and instead marks appropriate cooperative skills he/she observes on the team. At the end of the class, this sheet is discussed with the other team members. Students quickly see the strengths and weaknesses of the group.

STUDENT AND GROUP ACCOUNTABILITY

GROUP ACCOUNTABILITY

Group accountability is a very important concept in cooperative learning. The students must realize that we succeed only when everyone succeeds; thus the teacher must have methods and techniques for validating group accountability. One of the best methods for achieving group accountability is accepting a consensus assignment. Each team is responsible for turning in only one paper. The reporter will record all answers on this sheet; then the team must agree on the answers. Everyone in the group will receive this paper's grade.

Group accountability is also achieved by using a group point system. Before students were assigned to cooperative groups, the teacher had to determine a base score. This score is usually the last report card grade or last year's average. The base score is important not only for assigning students to teams but also for earning team points. The students earn points for the team based on this chart.

Test Score or Individual Paper	Points Earned for Group
A perfect score	3
10 or more points above the base score	3
5 to 9 points above the base score	2
4 points above to 4 points below the base score	1
5 or more points below the base score	0

Points are kept over a grading period, and the team with the highest total points receives some type of reward. Only the teacher can determine what he/she is willing to give as a reward and what would truly be rewarding to the students.

Assigning points encourages the students to strive for personal improvement all year. It also encourages peer tutoring on the teams because each member of the team needs to do well on tests and individual assignments in order for the team to score points.

The teacher may also want to assign team points if every member of the team has completed homework assignments. Another possibility is to assign team points for the use of appropriate cooperative skills when working on a team.

FEEDBACK

GRADES

A system of grading cooperative group work does include considerable change for the teacher. When assigning grades it is important that a spirit of interdependence be fostered. It tends to surprise students when they grasp the concept that everyone in the group got the same score. Complaints like, "John didn't do as much as I did," may be heard. This is the teacher's opportunity to state that when a group assignment is graded, everyone receives the same grade. Thus, it is up to the group to have total participation.

Low achieving students are often surprised to find that they received a high score. This occurrence can be a turning point in a child's self-esteem. It also tends to bring this low achieving child into the group activity more. He/she discovers the value of learning cooperatively.

In a cooperative environment, it is also important to grade work done independently after the group has practiced a particular skill.

One very workable format for cooperative learning follows:
- Provide direct instruction in the skill.
- Do a cooperative activity in which the skill is practiced.
- Individually quiz the students about the skill.

In another successful method, the teacher allows the students to complete a practice test cooperatively and then administers the actual test individually.

VERBAL PRAISE

Teachers must be aware of a valuable tool. This strategy is free and available to each teacher. This lifesaving technique is verbal praise. It works! Monitor cooperative groups, and when a good question is asked, a student helps another student, a good climate is being set in the group, or interdependence is being fostered, verbally praise the behavior. Cooperative learning is new to the students, and they are unsure of the norms of behavior. Help the class by bringing attention to the great things happening in the room.

If verbal praise is difficult for the teacher, "Twenty Ways To Say 'Good Cooperative Work!'" on page 27 provides ideas and suggestions for praise. If a teacher feels fake giving verbal praise, he/she should keep in mind that it is a new technique and just takes practice.

FEEDBACK

WALL CHART

An effective method for integrating cooperative learning in the classroom is a wall chart. The chart should include the names of each group and its members. The student roles should be included, along with the bonus points accrued by each team. Post bonus points on the chart, and watch the students gather around the chart like bees after honey.

HOW TO REWARD COOPERATIVE GROUPS

Most school systems and school teachers experience budget problems. Money is generally not available for class rewards. Listed below are a dozen rewards that could be used in the class.

- Free time - Allow five to ten minutes of free time to play a computer game, sit with friends, or play a board game.
- A trip to the soft drink machine - Students must supply the money.
- Homework passes - A slip of paper that states it can be exchanged for a missing assignment.
- A free "100" on a homework assignment - A slip of paper that states that it can be exchanged for a poor grade on an assignment.
- A certificate - Many software programs print simple certificates.
- A field trip - The teacher may be able to walk with the class to a local fast food restaurant, etc.
- A soft drink and chip party - Tell the class to bring soft drinks and snacks, and the teacher can supply the cups and napkins.
- Special privilege time - On a particular day, the students can chew gum or drink soft drinks during class.
- A trip to the mall - After school, the teacher may take a cooperative group to the mall for one hour.
- Promotional materials - Be on the lookout for free materials at local businesses. (State you are a teacher and beg!)
- Grab bag - Clean out your desk, rummage through garage sales, pick up cheap tokens, or watch for sales, and create a box of goodies from which the students can choose.
- A trip to the gym or outside - Schedule a brief time in the gym to engage in intramural sports.

CLOSURE OF THE COOPERATIVE GROUPS

CLOSING ACTIVITIES

It is imperative that processing be included at the end of each cooperative group activity. Allow five to ten minutes at the close of the class period to evaluate the activity. A group processing inventory is one example of a closure activity. Other methods of closure include the following:

☞ Students demonstrate the new skill.

☞ A game activity - See "Every Which Way But 'Lose.'"

☞ A class discussion that begins with the statement, "The best cooperative thing we did today was _____ ."

☞ A quiz over the material.

☞ Students verbally praise fellow group members, shake hands, or pat each other on the back.

☞ Students discuss the target cooperative behaviors. Were quiet voices used? Did we perform our roles?

☞ Students review the teacher's monitoring checklist and student observer's data.

☞ Students list one thing they learned that day in the group.

☞ Students compose a song, rap, or riddle about cooperative learning.

COOPERATIVE COMMENTS

20 WAYS TO SAY "GOOD COOPERATIVE WORK!"

1. I like the way you made that comment.
2. Everyone is involved in this group – good.
3. This group is really organized. Each person is doing his/her job.
4. I like the way you shared that last answer.
5. Good, you understand that question. Now show Tim.
6. You made this tough assignment look easy.
7. That's a great way to ask a question!
8. I think you are better at explaining that than I am.
9. Smart group! Smart group!
10. Thanks for explaining your answer to the group.
11. Together you are a genius.
12. That was a great way to get everybody involved.
13. That's an interesting point of view.
14. I can see you all have mastered that skill.
15. This group is impressive.
16. I'm glad you reminded the group about that rule.
17. That's a creative way to tackle the assignment.
18. You all have accomplished a lot today.
19. That was a great discussion on question 4.
20. Super cooperative behavior!

Remember...
Be specific.
Be positive.
Reinforce your norms for behavior.
Reinforce interpersonal skills.

OBSERVATION FORM

TEACHER OBSERVATION SHEET

Observation Date _____ / _____ / _____

INSTRUCTIONS:

- Choose one or two cooperative skills for observation. (See "Group Processing Skills," pages 15-16, for a suggested list of cooperative skills.)
- Write the skills you will observe on the chart below. Stand by each group for one minute; then move to the next group and observe.
- Record each use of the skill with a tally in the box under the skill.
- Under comments, note any outstanding examples of using the pinpointed skill(s). Later, share the comments with individual groups.

Team Number	Cooperative Skill	Cooperative Skill	Comments
Team 1			
Team 2			
Team 3			
Team 4			
Team 5			
Team 6			

OBSERVATION FORM

STUDENT OBSERVATION SHEET

Observation Date _____ / _____ / _____

INSTRUCTIONS:

- From the list below, choose one cooperative skill for observation.
  - listening
  - using quiet voices
  - summarizing
  - explaining answers
  - contributing ideas
  - staying on task

- Under cooperative skill, mark tallies every time a student uses this skill.
- Under comments, record any outstanding examples of a teammate using this skill.

Names of Teammates	Cooperative Skill	Comments
1. _____		
2. _____		
3. _____		
4. _____		
5. _____		
6. _____		

BLUEPRINT FOR MATH

SUBJECT AREA: Mathematics

SKILL: Any math skill that can be taught with a work sheet or a page from the textbook.

OBJECTIVE: The students will assist each other with a new math skill.

MATERIALS:
- Math textbook or math work sheet
- Paper
- Pencil

SUGGESTION FOR POSITIVE INTERDEPENDENCE: Students may use individual books or work sheets, but only one copy of the work should be turned in. All members must agree on the final paper turned in.

SUGGESTIONS FOR ACCOUNTABILITY:
- *Group:* All students will be responsible for the answers on the final cooperative paper.
- *Individual:* The individual students will be asked to do a similar skill on their own.

Necessary Knowledge: The teacher should directly instruct the class on the specific skill.

Cooperative Collaboration: Students are assigned a work sheet or a page from the text to do cooperatively. Each student may use his/her own book or work sheet, but the group must turn in only one assignment. All students must sign their name to the group assignment. Signing the assignment means that all students agree with the answers and are willing to accept the grade on the cooperative assignment.

Grand Finale: After the cooperative assignment is complete, students are then required to do a follow-up assignment on their own. Teachers could assign the even problems on a page in the textbook as a cooperative activity. Then, the odd problems could be assigned as an individual homework assignment.

Next time I plan to _____

_____

THE THINKING "T"

SUBJECT AREA: Mathematics

GRADE LEVEL: 5-9

OBJECTIVE: Students will improve visualization skills.

MATERIALS:
- A "Tangram I" work sheet (pages 32-33) for every two students.
- Enough tangrams (page 34) for every two students to have a set.

SUGGESTION FOR POSITIVE INTERDEPENDENCE:
Allow teams to divide into pairs to solve the puzzles. If one pair becomes stuck, they may consult the other members of their team.

SUGGESTIONS FOR ACCOUNTABILITY:
- *Group:* Each group must turn in a work sheet.
- *Individual:* Call on different individuals to show their solutions on the chalkboard or the overhead projector.

Necessary Knowledge: None

Cooperative Collaboration: Students will complete the work sheet for "Tangram I."

Grand Finale:
- Call on different students to show their solutions on the overhead projector or the chalkboard.
- Give each student a package of tangrams and let him/her solve a new puzzle.

Next time I plan to _____

_____

THE THINKING "T"

TANGRAM I WORK SHEET

Question 1
A. Use the seven tangram pieces to make a square. When you have discovered the answer, draw your solution in the square marked 1 on the "Tangram I."

Question 2
A. Use the seven tangram pieces to make a triangle. When you have discovered the answer, draw your solution in the triangle marked 2A on the "Tangram I."
B. Can the seven tangram pieces be rearranged to make another triangle? If so, draw that solution in the triangle marked 2B on the "Tangram I."

Question 3
Arrange the seven tangram pieces to make the shape marked 3. When you have discovered the answer, draw your solution in the shape.

Enrichment
Using the seven tangram pieces, discover what other shapes you can make. Draw these arrangements on the back of the work sheet.

THE THINKING "T"

TANGRAM I WORK SHEET

1.

2A.   2B.

3.

© 1991 by Incentive Publications, Inc., Nashville, TN

Names _____

THE THINKING "T"

TANGRAM PATTERNS

YEAH FOR YARN!

SUBJECT AREA: Mathematics

GRADE LEVEL: 5-9

OBJECTIVE:
- Students will practice using their knowledge about geometric shapes.
- Students will develop their thinking skills.
- Students will improve spatial perception.

MATERIALS: One 6 yard loop of yarn for each team, plus all necessary work sheets.

SUGGESTION FOR POSITIVE INTERDEPENDENCE: Each student should have both hands touching the yarn.

SUGGESTIONS FOR ACCOUNTABILITY:
- *Group:* The teacher will notice, acknowledge, and praise success.
- *Individual:* Students will answer a quiz on geometric shape names.

Necessary Knowledge: Students should be introduced to the following vocabulary: triangle, hexagon, equilateral, rectangle, decagon, congruent, parallelogram, isosceles, similar, trapezoid, scalene, quadrilateral, square, rhombus, pentagon, heptagon, octagon, and nonagon.

Cooperative Collaboration: Students must cooperate in order to build the figures.

Grand Finale: Students will take a quiz on geometric terms.

Next time I plan to _____

_____

YEAH FOR YARN!

INSTRUCTION SHEET FOR THE TEACHER

1. Students are grouped in teams, with one yarn loop per team.

2. Students are required to keep both hands on the yarn at all times. Students may need to also use hands, teeth, etc., to form some of these shapes. Students are encouraged to share knowledge with each other about how to build each shape in the simplest manner. Remind students they will have a quiz over these terms at the end of this class. It is the responsibility of each team member to be sure that all team members know these terms at the end of this activity.

3. The teacher should ask the groups to form certain geometric shapes. The teacher should circulate among the teams, and as each team successfully shows its shape, the teacher assigns another slightly more difficult task. If the team does not have any members able to help form the shape, the teacher may assist with the necessary knowledge.

4. The following are suggestions for figures the teacher may ask teams to demonstrate:

triangle	heptagon
quadrilateral	octagon
square	nonagon
rectangle	decagon
parallelogram	equilateral triangle
rhombus	isosceles triangle
trapezoid	scalene triangle
pentagon	three equilateral triangles
hexagon	
three quadrilaterals that are not rectangles	four congruent triangles

YEAH FOR YARN!

QUIZ

Name the geometric figure that has:

1. Ten sides _____

2. Eight sides _____

3. Six sides _____

4. Three sides _____

5. Nine sides _____

6. Seven sides _____

7. Five sides _____

8. Four congruent sides with the opposite sides parallel _____

9. Four sides with the opposite sides congruent and parallel _____

10. Three congruent sides _____

*Answer Key

Names _____

PRIME TIME

SUBJECT AREA: Mathematics

GRADE LEVEL: 5-9

OBJECTIVES: Students will learn to identify factors, common factors, and prime and composite numbers.

MATERIALS:
- One work sheet (page 39) for each team
- Twelve small wooden cubes for each team
- "Sieve of Eratosthenes" work sheet (page 40) for each student
- Colored pencils

SUGGESTION FOR POSITIVE INTERDEPENDENCE:
Each student should work the cube activity to be sure everyone in the group agrees on the answers.

SUGGESTIONS FOR ACCOUNTABILITY:
- *Group:* Everyone in the group must agree on the answers for the cube work sheet. Only one work sheet will be turned in for each team, and all team members will receive that grade.
- *Individual:* Each student will individually work the "Sieve of Eratosthenes" work sheet and turn that in for an individual grade. Students will be given a work sheet to identify factors and common factors and prime and composite numbers. Students should work these individually and receive individual grades, as well as team points, for this work.

Necessary Knowledge: Students need to know what a factor is and what a rectangle is.

Cooperative Collaboration: The students should work the cube work sheet together. Students will work the "Sieve of Eratosthenes" work sheet individually, but still in groups, and may help each other if they become confused.

Grand Finale:
Students return to their individual seats and finish a work sheet identifying factors, common factors, and prime and composite numbers.

Next time I plan to _____

_____

PRIME TIME

1. Build as many rectangles as possible using two to twelve cubes, and record your results on this chart.

Number of Blocks	Different Widths	Number of Widths

2. What do you notice about the relationship of the number of blocks to the different widths?

_____

3. What are some common factors of 2 and 4?_____
   - 3 and 9? _____
   - 6 and 12? _____

4. What is the greatest common factor of 3 and 12? _____
   - 2 and 6? _____
   - 8 and 12? _____
   - 7 and 3? _____

5. Look on your chart and circle the numbers that have exactly two widths. These numbers are called prime numbers. What can you tell about the relationship between the blocks that are prime numbers and the number of widths? _____

6. Look on your chart at the numbers that aren't circled. These are called composite numbers. What can you tell about the relationship between composite numbers and the number of widths? _____

_____

Names _____

© 1991 by Incentive Publications, Inc., Nashville, TN

PRIME TIME

THE SIEVE OF ERATOSTHENES

STEP 1: Cross off 1.

STEP 2: Circle 2, and using colored pencils, shade in every number that is evenly divisible by 2.

STEP 3: Circle 3 and shade in every number that is evenly divisible by 3.

STEP 4: Circle 5 and shade in every number that is evenly divisible by 5.

STEP 5: Circle 7 and shade in every number that is evenly divisible by 7.

1	2	3	4	5	6	7	8	9	10
11	12	13	14	15	16	17	18	19	20
21	22	23	24	25	26	27	28	29	30
31	32	33	34	35	36	37	38	39	40
41	42	43	44	45	46	47	48	49	50
51	52	53	54	55	56	57	58	59	60
61	62	63	64	65	66	67	68	69	70
71	72	73	74	75	76	77	78	79	80
81	82	83	84	85	86	87	88	89	90
91	92	93	94	95	96	97	98	99	100

The numbers that are not shaded are prime numbers.
The numbers that are shaded are composite numbers.

Names _____

COOPERATIVE SOUP

SUBJECT AREA: Mathematics

GRADE LEVEL: 5-9

SKILLS:
- Reading and doubling a recipe
- Practicing with customary measures
- Practicing the cooperative skill of interdependence

OBJECTIVES:
- The class will prepare soup while following a recipe.
- The cooperative groups complete a work sheet on customary measures.
- The students will listen to the story *Stone Soup,* and the students will discuss how cooperative behavior was exhibited in this folktale.

MATERIALS:
- The ingredients for a vegetable soup recipe (see example on page 42)
- A crock pot or any pot and heating device
- Student work sheet for "Cooperative Soup"
- The story *Stone Soup* by Ann McGovern (Scholastic, Inc.)
- Spoons and cups for serving the soup
- Any other kitchen utensils necessary to prepare the soup

SUGGESTION FOR POSITIVE INTERDEPENDENCE:

Assign cooperative groups portions of the recipe to assemble. Remind the class that in order to have a tasty "brew," everyone must contribute.

SUGGESTIONS FOR ACCOUNTABILITY:
- *Group:* The group must work cooperatively to complete their portion of the "Cooperative Soup."
- *Individual:* Each group member must be accountable for a portion of the recipe the group has been assigned. Each member must contribute information to help complete the work sheet.

Necessary Knowledge: Students need a basic understanding of customary units (cups, pints, teaspoon, etc.).

Cooperative Collaboration: The students will practice group interdependence by completing their group's portion of "Cooperative Soup," and the class will have a sense of classwide interdependence when the soup is finished.

Grand Finale: The students will have a tangible product of their cooperative efforts; they can enjoy the cooperative soup! A soup party is in order after the assignment.

A quiz can be given on how to double a recipe and other facts dealing with customary conversions.

COOPERATIVE SOUP

Suggested Recipe for Cooperative Soup

1 c. frozen green beans
1 c. frozen vegetable mix
1 c. chopped onion
1 c. chopped celery
1 clove garlic
3 T. oil
5 poultry bouillon cubes
5 c. water

28 oz. can tomatoes, cut up, drained
6 oz. tomato paste
1 c. chopped carrots
1 c. chopped potatoes
2 t. sugar
1 t. basil leaves
1 t. thyme leaves
4 oz. spaghetti noodles

Saute onions, celery, and garlic in oil until tender. Stir in all other ingredients except spaghetti. Bring to a boil, reduce heat. Simmer until the vegetables are tender. Stir in spaghetti and cook an additional ten minutes. Makes 10-15 small servings.

SUGGESTIONS:
- If the students are young, have them bring the vegetables already cut up!
- Assign cooperative groups certain ingredients to bring from home.
- Read *Stone Soup* to the class as the soup simmers. Then discuss the cooperative behaviors seen in the book.

Next time I plan to _____

_____

_____

COOPERATIVE SOUP

Double and rewrite the following recipe:

Original Ingredients
1 c. frozen green beans
1 clove of garlic
28 oz. of tomatoes
6 oz. tomato paste
2 t. sugar
3 T. oil

Doubled Ingredients
_____
_____
_____
_____
_____
_____

Write the word that each abbreviation represents.

1). c._____   5). T. _____

2). t._____   6). oz._____

3). lb._____   7). pt. _____

4). qt._____   8). gal. _____

In each blank write teaspoon(s), cup(s), quarts(s), or gallon(s).

1. A typical dosage of cough syrup for a child is 2 _____ .

2. A glass of orange juice is 1 _____ .

3. A recipe calls for 1 _____ of salt.

4. The cookie recipe calls for 2 _____ of sugar.

5. The punch recipe calls for 2 _____ of water.

Complete.
1). 1 c. _____ oz.   4). 2 gal. _____ qt.   7). 6 c. _____ pt.
2). 1 T. _____ t.   5). 3 c. _____ oz.   8). 1 lb. _____ oz.
3). 3 qt. _____ pt.   6). 16 oz. _____ lb.   9). 2 c. _____ oz.

Enrichment
If Cooperative Soup yields 1 gallon of soup and there are 24 students in the class,
how many ounces of soup will each student receive? _____

_____

*Answer Key
Names _____

CONFUSED ABOUT CONVEX?

SUBJECT AREA: Mathematics

GRADE LEVEL: 7-9

OBJECTIVES:
- Students will learn how to use geoboards.
- Students will discover a rule to find the sum of the measures of the angles of convex polygons.

MATERIALS:
- One geoboard for every two students
- Rubber bands
- One work sheet for every two students

SUGGESTION FOR POSITIVE INTERDEPENDENCE:
Allow teams to divide into pairs to solve the work sheet. If one pair of students has difficulty, they may consult the other members of their team.

SUGGESTIONS FOR ACCOUNTABILITY:
- *Group:* Each group must turn in a work sheet.
- *Individual:* At the end of the class period, ask each student to individually find the sum of the measure of the angles of a heptagon.

Necessary Knowledge:
- Students need to know how to use geoboards.
- Students need to know these vocabulary words: vertex, pentagon, diagonal, hexagon, triangle, octagon, quadrilateral, and heptagon.

Cooperative Collaboration: The students will use the work sheet to discover the rule.

Grand Finale:
Ask each student to individually find the sum of the measure of the angles of a heptagon. The students should write the answer on notebook paper.

Next time I plan to _____

_____

CONFUSED ABOUT CONVEX?

Determining the sum of the measures of the angles of convex polygons:

1. Build a four-sided polygon on the geoboard. Put a rubber band over the peg at any vertex and stretch it to the peg at an opposite vertex. A line connecting two vertices that are not next to each other is called a diagonal. Can you make another diagonal starting at the same vertex? _____

2. Fill in the following chart by building the polygons and finding the number of diagonals that can be drawn from each vertex. When you finish, leave the octagon and its diagonals on your board.

Polygon	Number Of Sides	Number Of Diagonals From One Vertex
Triangle	3	
Quadrilateral	4	
Pentagon	5	
Hexagon	6	
Octagon	8	

• What is the relationship between the numbers of diagonals from one vertex and the number of sides in a polygon? _____

_____

• How many diagonals are in a 10-sided polygon? _____
• How many diagonals are in a 50-sided polygon? _____

3. What shapes are made inside the octagon on your geoboard? _____

_____

• How many triangles are inside this polygon? _____

Names _____

© 1991 by Incentive Publications, Inc., Nashville, TN

CONFUSED ABOUT CONVEX?

Fill in the following chart by building the polygons and marking the diagonals to determine the number of triangles on your geoboard.

Polygon	Number Of Sides	Number Of Triangles
Triangle		
Quadrilateral		
Pentagon		
Hexagon		
Octagon		

- What is the relationship between the number of triangles and the number of sides? _____
- How many triangles are in a 10-sided polygon? _____
- How many triangles are in a 50-sided polygon? _____

4. Are all the angles of the octagon part of a triangle? _____
   What is the sum of the angles of a triangle? _____
   How many triangles are in an octagon? _____
   So, what is the the sum of the angles of an octagon?

   _____

Now fill in the following chart.

Polygon	Number Of Triangles	Sum Of All The Angles
Triangle		
Quadrilateral		
Pentagon		
Hexagon		
Octagon		

Names _____

© 1991 by Incentive Publications, Inc., Nashville, TN

MEAN, MEDIAN, MODE, AND ME!

SUBJECT AREA: Mathematics

GRADE LEVEL: 5-9

OBJECTIVE: Students will find mean, median, mode, and range.

MATERIALS:
- "Mean, Median, Mode, and Me" student page
- "Mean, Median, Mode, and Me" data sheet
- Candy coated chocolate candies
- Paper towels

SUGGESTION FOR POSITIVE INTERDEPENDENCE: The group data will require the students to function dependently.

SUGGESTIONS FOR ACCOUNTABILITY:
- *Group:* Each group is responsible for turning in a data sheet.
- *Individual:* Each student must find the mean, median, mode, and range for his/her candy coated chocolate candies.

Necessary Knowledge: Introduction to mean, median, mode, and range.

Cooperative Collaboration: Students will complete the data sheet as a group.

Grand Finale:
- Groups that have successfully completed the data sheet may enjoy their candy!
- Students can discuss the statistical information they discovered. How were the packages similar? How were they different?

Next time I plan to _____

_____

MEAN, MEDIAN, MODE, AND ME!

HOW TO FIND...
- **Mean:** Add the numbers; then divide by the number of addends. example: $1 + 2 + 3 = 6$; $6 \div 3 = 2$; 2 is the **mean.**
- **Median:** Place the numbers in order from largest to smallest. The number in the middle is the **median.**
- **Mode:** The mode is the number that occurs most often. Sometimes there is no mode; sometimes there is more than one **mode.**
- **Range:** Subtract the smallest number from the largest number to find the **range.**

Steps 1 through 5 are done individually with each person's own candy.

Step 1: Each student counts the candy in his/her package. Record this number on the data sheet. Using a paper towel, line up the candy in order from the color that there is the most of to the color there is the least of in the package. Example:

Step 2: Mean (average) – Each member counts the total number of pieces of candy in the package. Divide by the number of colors in each package. Record each group member's **mean** on the data sheet.

Step 3: Mode – Write the color of each group member's **mode** on the data sheet.

Names _____

MEAN, MEDIAN, MODE, AND ME!

Step 4: Median - Write the **median** of the chocolate candies. This can be determined by looking at the candies that are in order on the paper towel. Which color is in the middle? There may be two colors with the same number; if so, write both colors on the data sheet.

Step 5: Range - Write the **range** of the colors on the data sheet.

For Steps 6 through 10, combine the group's chocolate candies.

Step 6: On the data sheet record the **total number** of chocolate candies in all the packages.

Step 7: What was the **mean** number of chocolate candies in the group's packages? Record this information on the data sheet.

Step 8: What is the color of the **mode** of chocolate candies in the group's packages? Write the color for the mode on the data sheet. If there is more than one mode, list all mode colors.

Step 9: What is the group's **median** color? Write the answer on the data sheet.

Step 10: What is the group's **range** of chocolate candies? Write the number on the data sheet.

ENRICHMENT
1. Draw a bar graph illustrating a statistical fact about chocolate candies. Use colored pencils or markers to add color to the graph.
2. Write to the manufacturer of the chocolate candies to discover why certain colors are used more often than other colors.

Names _____

Mean, median, mode, and Me!
DATA SHEET

Name	Step 1 Total Candies	Step 2 Mean Color	Step 3 Mode Color	Step 4 Median Color	Step 5 Range

Group Data	Step 6 Total Candies	Step 7 Group Mean	Step 8 Group Mode	Step 9 Group Median	Step 10 Group Range

ENRICHMENT GRAPH:

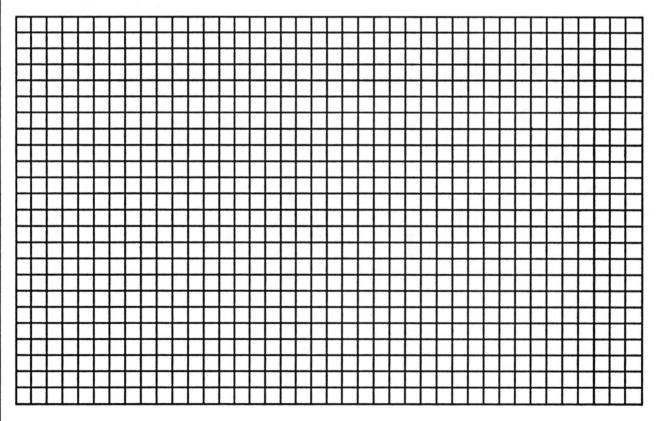

Names _____

BLUEPRINT FOR LANGUAGE

SUBJECT AREA: Language Arts

OBJECTIVES: To implement cooperative learning using existing textbooks and materials in the language arts classroom.

SUGGESTIONS FOR POSITIVE INTERDEPENDENCE:
Provide direct instruction in the specific skill. Assign a work sheet for cooperative group work; then assign a similar activity for individual homework.

Provide direct instruction in the specific skill. Assign the first half of the assignment to be completed in cooperative groups and the second half of the assignment to be completed individually.

Assign a specific assignment to a cooperative group consisting of two students. The students work together on the assignment, but only one paper is turned in. Both group members must agree on the answers. Both students would receive the same grade.

When preparing for a test, e.g., a test over the plural forms of words, the cooperative groups meet together and devise quizzes or games to help prepare the entire group for the upcoming test. Flash cards, practice sheets, student-made games, etc., could be used.

SUGGESTIONS FOR ACCOUNTABILITY:
- *Group:* The groups would receive the same grade on cooperative assignments. Then on the individual assignments, the individual would earn group points. (See student and group accountability sections, pages 22 and 23, for a discussion on cooperative group points.)
- *Individual:* A follow-up assignment or quiz would assess the individual's progress on the particular skill.

Necessary Knowledge: The teacher provides instruction in the prerequisites needed for the particular lesson being taught.

Cooperative Collaboration: Students will be assigned a specific task to do cooperatively. Hopefully, a model of peer tutoring will be implemented in the group activity so that the entire group will be able to achieve a mastery level of performance on the specific assigned skill.

Grand Finale: A test or quiz could be given over the specific skill to assess class progress.

Next time I plan to _____

BLUEPRINT FOR SPELLING

SUBJECT AREA: Spelling

GRADE LEVEL: All grades

OBJECTIVE: Students will learn how to spell the weekly spelling words.

MATERIALS: Spelling textbook for each student

SUGGESTIONS FOR POSITIVE INTERDEPENDENCE:
- Divide the words evenly among the students on each team. Each student is responsible for teaching his/her word to the other members of his/her team.
- If every member of a team masters the weekly spelling words, the team receives a reward. If one or more team members do not show mastery, the team does not receive a reward.

SUGGESTIONS FOR ACCOUNTABILITY:
- *Group:* The group will receive a reward if every member of the group masters the spelling words.
- *Individual:* The student receives his/her individual spelling test score.

Necessary Knowledge: The teacher spends the first two days giving a pretest and teaching from the spelling book.

Cooperative Collaboration:
- Students spend the third day developing games and activities to teach the words to each other.
- Students spend the fourth day playing the games or going through the activities.

Grand Finale: The teacher gives the final spelling test. Each student receives an individual spelling grade. The teacher rewards any teams that have every student scoring 100 on the final spelling test.

Next time I plan to _____

_____

WHO, WHAT, WHEN, AND WHERE?

SUBJECT AREA:
- Language Arts
- Social Studies
- Science

GRADE LEVEL: 5-9

SKILL:
- Students will be required to find specific information.
- Students will understand how to summarize material.

OBJECTIVE: Cooperative groups will be given newspaper articles, handouts, or weekly newsletters (*Weekly Reader, Scholastic Magazine*, etc.). As a group they will read the articles; then the students will locate the "who, what, when, and where" of each reading.

MATERIALS:
- 4 different articles for the cooperative activity. (Each group should have a copy of each of the articles.)
- 1 article per class member for the individual follow-up activity.
- A "Who, What, When, and Where" quiz sheet.
- 4 markers, colored pencils, or crayons per group (red, blue, black, and green)

SUGGESTIONS FOR POSITIVE INTERDEPENDENCE:
The cooperative group should consist of four members. When the students are in their groups, the teacher numbers the students off by 1, 2, 3, and 4. Using the first article, the 1s are responsible for finding the "who" in the article and marking it with the red marker; the 2s are responsible for finding the "what" in the article and marking it with the blue marker; the 3s are responsible for finding the "when" in the article and marking it with the black marker; the 4s are responsible for finding the "where" and marking it with the green marker. After this article is complete, the group discusses their choices. After agreement has been reached, one article is marked with all the colors that identify the "who, what, when, and where." Then together the group writes a short summary of the article.

WHO, WHAT, WHEN, AND WHERE?

Before reading the next article, each group member hands his/her marker to the person to the right. The person holding the color listed below is now responsible for finding the particular portion that goes with that color marker.

- Red Marker = Who
- Blue Marker = What
- Black Marker = When
- Green Marker = Where

Continue in the same fashion until all articles have been marked and each student has had the opportunity to find who, what, when, and where. Four summaries should also be completed.

SUGGESTIONS FOR ACCOUNTABILITY:

- *Group:* Each group member must be able to identify his/her particular section of the articles.
- *Individual:* At the close of the cooperative lessons, each student will have an article in which he/she will have to find the "who, what, when, and where" on his/her own.

Necessary Knowledge: To prepare for this lesson, the teacher should do a similar article with the entire class.

Cooperative Collaboration: Students must be responsible for their particular portion. The group will summarize the articles cooperatively.

Grand Finale: Students will individually complete an article where they will have to identify who, what, when, and where. They will then write a summary of the article.

Next time I plan to _____

_____

WHO, WHAT, WHEN, AND WHERE?

QUIZ

Read the article the teacher has given you. Then answer the following questions.

1. Write the "who" of the article _____

_____

2. Write the "what" of the article _____

_____

3. Write the "when" of the article _____

_____

4. Write the "where" of the article _____

_____

5. Write a brief summary of your article _____

_____

_____

_____

_____

_____

_____

_____

Names _____

DON'T CATCH COMMA FEVER!

SUBJECT AREA: Language Arts

GRADE LEVEL: 4-9

SKILL: The students will practice using commas correctly.

OBJECTIVE: A work sheet on the correct use of the comma will be completed by each cooperative group.

MATERIALS:
- Pencil
- "Comma Fever" rule sheet (or a language textbook that contains the rules for comma placement)
- "Comma Fever" work sheet

SUGGESTION FOR POSITIVE INTERDEPENDENCE:
To ensure more interdependence for this activity, the cooperative groups should consist of two members. If necessary pair off an existing larger cooperative group of four into two teams of two.

SUGGESTIONS FOR ACCOUNTABILITY:
- *Group:* Students must be taught by the group the rules for correct comma placement.
- *Individual:* The teacher should observe the class to ensure all members are contributing to the assignment. Students should be told that following the cooperative group activity, an individual assignment or test will be given over the rules of comma placement. It is the cooperative group's responsibility to make sure each member understands the rules for commas. (On the follow-up assignment, an option would be to give all students the assignment/test and grade only one paper per group.)

Necessary Knowledge: Students must be able to identify a comma.

Cooperative Collaboration: The students will discuss correct comma placement on the activity sheet.

Grand Finale: Students will complete an individual test or assignment to demonstrate comma placement skill.

Teacher's Note: This lesson format could be used with the regular language arts textbook.

Next time I plan to _____

DON'T CATCH COMMA FEVER!

Rules for Correct Comma Usage

Rule 1: Use commas to separate items in a series.

- *Example: June, July, and August are Ms. Smith's favorite months.*

Rule 2: Use a comma before conjunctions when they join the parts of a compound sentence. (Common conjunctions are *and, but, nor, for,* and *yet.*)

- *Example: I went to the store, and Jim went to the restaurant.*

Rule 3: Use commas to set off expressions that interrupt the sentence.

- *Example: Mrs. Noname, our teacher, is very nice.*

Rule 4: Use commas to separate items in dates.

- *Example: July 4, 1990.*

Rule 5: Use commas to separate items in addresses.

- *Example: Nashville, Tennessee*

Rule 6: Use a comma after the salutation of a handwritten friendly letter.

- *Example: Dear John,*

Rule 7: Use a comma after the closing of any letter.

- *Example: Sincerely,*

Names _____

DON'T CATCH COMMA FEVER!

When it comes to commas, students often catch "comma fever." This is a very common disease that affects middle school students. It is deadly to a sentence. Please avoid this dreaded disease. It will plague you to failure. The first symptom of this dangerous fever could be a failing grade on a language arts assignment. If it is not cured immediately, a student's language arts report card grade drops to a dangerous level. The worst part of the disease is that parents may begin to request that their child spend one hour a night studying language arts. (This hour occurs when a favorite television show is on.) Please be careful and avoid this disease. Always have a reason to place a comma!

With your cooperative group member, place commas correctly in each sentence. Write the rule you used in your decision to place the comma. A score of 90 percent will ensure that the comma disease has not invaded your mind…yet!

1. I live in Nashville Tennessee.

Rule _____

2. She was born on August 29 1955 and now she lives in Columbus Ohio.

Rule _____

Rule _____

Rule _____

3. Joe Smith the mailman lives two blocks away.

Rule _____

4. June July August and September are the summer months.

Rule _____

5. What did you tell the doctor Jane?

Rule _____

6. Please forward all my mail to 331 Anywhere Drive Nashville Tennessee.

Rule _____

7. John went to school in Dallas Texas and Bill went to school in Boise Idaho.

Rule _____

Rule _____

Rule _____

8. Florida a favorite vacation spot is a beautiful state.

Rule _____

9. Lincoln was shot on April 14 1865 in Washington D.C.

Rule _____

Rule _____

Names _____

© 1991 by Incentive Publications, Inc., Nashville, TN

DON'T CATCH COMMA FEVER!

10. She was going to call her mother but she forgot.

Rule _____

11. Karen was supposed to buy butter cheese milk and ice cream.

Rule _____

12. I went to Dr. Smith a famous brain surgeon to get relief from comma fever.

Rule _____

13. Bill Mary Joe Helen and I went to the football game.

Rule _____

14. Mary do you have a dime?

Rule _____

15. My mother lives in San Diego California.

Rule _____

In the following letter, place commas correctly.

331 Anywhere
Nashville Tennessee 11111
July 4 1990

Dear Sam

   I just can't believe it! Dr. Art a famous physician said I have comma fever. My first hint of the disease came when I did not bother learning my rules for commas. Soon I an "A" student was putting commas everywhere! Commas periods semicolons and exclamation marks were everywhere on my paper. My grades declined in language arts. As my fever went up my grades went down. My grades were 80 77 66 50 and 42. I got a 32 and my mother grounded me. Please come by and see me. Sam bring my language arts book my reading book and my spelling book. Dr. Art my physician said studying my lessons is the only cure.

Your feverish friend

Fred

SPELLING DEMONS

SUBJECT AREA: Spelling

GRADE LEVEL: 4-7

OBJECTIVE: Students will learn how to spell difficult spelling words.

MATERIALS: List of "Spelling Demon" words, plus other necessary work sheets.

SUGGESTION FOR POSITIVE INTERDEPENDENCE:
Let each team divide the words evenly among themselves. Each student is then responsible for learning his/her words and for teaching these words to the rest of the team.

SUGGESTIONS FOR ACCOUNTABILITY:
- *Group:* After the final test, average the scores of the team members. Each member of the team receives that grade.
- *Individual:* Each student also receives an individual test grade based on his/her individual test score.

> **Necessary Knowledge:** The teacher will need to share many ideas for games to practice spelling words. The teacher will also need to have spelling rules available and appropriate strategies for learning these words.
>
> **Cooperative Collaboration:** Give each team a copy of the "Spelling Demon" list with the instructions to:
> 1. Divide the words evenly among themselves.
> 2. Learn the words themselves.
> 3. Devise games, activities, or strategies to teach these words to their teammates.
>
> **Grand Finale:**
> - Test
> - Spelling Bee

Next time I plan to _____

_____

SPELLING DEMONS

Activities for Learning Spelling Demon Words

1. Make word search puzzles for the other students to solve.

2. Make crossword puzzles for the other students to solve.

3. Round-Robin Drill - One child says a word he/she remembers and spells it. The next child repeats that word and then adds another word of his/her own. The third child repeats both and adds another one. This continues until one child misses; then begin again.

4. Scrambled Letters - Mix up the letters in each demon word and have the team members straighten them out to spell the word correctly.

5. Hangman - One student draws the spaces for each letter in a mystery demon word. Students take turns guessing letters that may fill in the spaces. If a student guesses a correct letter, the "student teacher" fills in the space. If a student guesses an incorrect letter, the "student teacher" draws a part of a man on the scaffold. This continues until the word is spelled correctly or the man is complete. If the word is spelled correctly, that student chooses the next word.

6. Students write stories using as many of the demon words as possible but leaving blank spaces where the demon words would be. Students exchange papers and try to correctly fill in the blank spaces. Be sure they spell the words correctly!

7. Write each word on a strip of paper, cut out each letter, and put the letters in an envelope. Pass around the envelopes and try to arrange the letters of the "demon word" correctly. Students check others' work against the demon word list.

SPELLING DEMONS

Student Instruction Sheet For Spelling Demons

This activity will take at least two days, maybe more.
- Spend the first day memorizing your own demon words.
- Spend the second day devising games, activities, or strategies to teach your words to your team members.
- Spend the rest of the days on this project playing the games you and your teammates have developed and completing the activity sheets you made.

Step 1: Divide "spelling demon words" evenly among team members.

Step 2: Each team member must memorize his/her own spelling demon words.

Step 3: Each team member must devise strategies, activities, or games to help the other team members learn the words.

Step 4: Take turns helping teammates learn the words by showing the strategy, working the activity, or playing the games that are devised.

Step 5: Give each other a practice test and check it so each student will know which words to study at home.

Step 6: Your teacher will give a final test to the group. Don't forget that not only is each team member responsible for knowing all the demon words, but you are also responsible for making sure that every member of your team knows these words. **Your grade depends on the success of your team.**

SPELLING DEMONS

Student List of Spelling Demons

ache	easy	since
again	every	straight
always	friend	sugar
answer	guess	sure
blue	half	tear
built	hour	through
busy	knew	tires
can't	know	tonight
color	laid	trouble
cough	minute	wear
could	often	where
country	ready	women
doctor	said	won't
does	says	write
don't	seems	
early	shoes	

JUST THE FACTS

SUBJECT AREA: Reading, science, or social studies

OBJECTIVE: To improve the skill of reading aloud, to improve listening, and to teach the skill of summarizing.

MATERIALS:
- Text consisting of at least 10 paragraphs
- "Just the Facts" work sheet

SUGGESTION FOR POSITIVE INTERDEPENDENCE:
A group of two is established. It is wise to mix a fluent reader and a less-fluent reader. The first child reads one paragraph to the other child. After the paragraph is read, the second student summarizes the paragraph in one or two sentences. Then the second student reads, and the first student summarizes the paragraph. The students can help each other decode or spell any words.

SUGGESTIONS FOR ACCOUNTABILITY:
- *Group:* Both members must take turns reading and summarizing.
- *Individual:* The individual student must do his/her specific role and assist his/her partner.

Necessary Knowledge: The student must be able to read and write.

Cooperative Collaboration: The cooperative group of two must work side by side on the entire assignment, and they must turn in one "Just the Facts" work sheet per group.

Grand Finale: The groups can share their summaries with the class. The teacher could select the summaries that were the most complete and concise.

Next time I plan to _____

_____

JUST THE FACTS

Step 1: Write the reading assignments you were given on the blank below.

_____

Step 2: With your partner you are to read and summarize each paragraph in this reading. First one student reads a paragraph to the other student. You can help each other out with the hard words. It is very important to listen carefully!

Step 3: The student that did not read the paragraph must write a one or two sentence summary of the paragraph. You can discuss the summary and help each other with the wording and the spelling. It is important to write the most important things. Remember, you are summarizing the paragraph.

Step 4: Now the student that summarized the first paragraph reads and the other student listens. Then the listener writes the summary. The group continues reading, taking turns reading and summarizing. Remember the teacher is looking for "just the facts."

Fill in the work sheet below as your cooperative group completes the activity.

Paragraph # 1
Summary_____
_____

Paragraph # 2
Summary_____
_____

Paragraph # 3
Summary_____
_____

Paragraph # 4
Summary_____
_____

Paragraph # 5
Summary_____
_____

Paragraph # 6
Summary_____
_____

Paragraph # 7
Summary_____
_____

Names _____

Just the Facts

Paragraph # 8
Summary_____
_____

Paragraph # 9
Summary_____
_____

Paragraph # 10
Summary_____
_____

Paragraph # 11
Summary_____
_____

Paragraph # 12
Summary_____
_____

Paragraph # 13
Summary_____
_____

(Use the back of this sheet if you have more than 13 paragraphs.)

Step 5: Working cooperatively, write a summary of all the paragraphs.
Remember, "just the facts"!

_____
_____
_____
_____
_____
_____

Step 6: If you could only use 20 words or less to summarize this reading,
what would you say? Write your summary below.

_____
_____
_____
_____
_____

Names _____

BURDEN OF PROOF

SUBJECT AREA: Language Arts

GRADE LEVEL: 5-9

OBJECTIVE: The students will learn how to proofread each other's work.

MATERIALS: Red pens, student instruction sheet

SUGGESTIONS FOR POSITIVE INTERDEPENDENCE:
1. Whenever the students write something, they will need to meet together in their cooperative learning groups to proofread each other's work.
2. The students will then rewrite the report making the appropriate corrections.

SUGGESTIONS FOR ACCOUNTABILITY:
- *Group:* The group knows that every student will be earning group points based on the individual score that the student earns. It would benefit the group for every student to score well on his/her report.
- *Individual:* Each individual student will receive an individual grade on his/her report.

Necessary Knowledge:
1. The students need to know how to spell and how to use a dictionary to look up spelling of unfamiliar words.
2. The students need to be familiar with comma usage rules.
3. The students need to know when to use capital letters.
4. The students need to know how to write effective sentences. The report needs to have unity and logical thinking.

Cooperative Collaboration: The students will proofread each other's work, explaining corrections if necessary.

Grand Finale:
Each student will turn in a corrected report for the teacher to read.

Next time I plan to _____

_____

BURDEN OF PROOF

Student Instruction Sheet

1. Every member of this team has finished writing a report. Before you turn it in, you need to ask your cooperative learning group to help you proofread your paper.

2. Everyone needs to pass his/her paper to the person on the left.

3. The Runner will check to be sure that commas and periods have been used correctly. If a comma or period needs to be removed, cross it out. If a comma or period needs to be added, do so.

4. The Checker needs to make sure all words are correctly spelled. If a word is misspelled, write the correct spelling above the misspelled word.

5. The Reporter needs to check all sentences to be sure they begin with capital letters. If any word needs to be capitalized and it isn't, circle the first letter in the word.

6. The Encourager needs to read the paper to be sure it has unity and logical thought. If there is any section of the paper that seems confusing or awkwardly worded, underline it in red pen and put a question mark next to it. When the writer gets this paper back, he/she will ask you what you didn't like about the part you marked, and he/she will ask for appropriate suggestions for corrections.

7. As each student finishes proofreading a paper, he/she passes it to the person on his/her left until he/she receives his/her own paper back.

8. Team members rewrite their papers making appropriate corrections and then turn in the finished product.

BLUEPRINT FOR SCIENCE

SUBJECT AREA: Science

GRADE LEVEL: 4-9

OBJECTIVE: Using the cooperative learning method, the teacher will devise new techniques for teaching science.

MATERIALS:
- Paper
- Pencil
- Text
- Resource materials

SUGGESTIONS FOR POSITIVE INTERDEPENDENCE:
- When the class is studying a broad topic (for example, a chapter or unit in the textbook), the teacher divides the topic into mini-topics. Each student on the team is assigned a mini-topic to research. One member from each team will work on this mini-topic, so the members will group together to research, write their reports, and decide how to teach it to the other team members. After the students have become "experts" on their mini-topics, they return to their teams to teach it to their teammates.
- Team members will proofread each other's reports.
- Team members will develop a creative project incorporating the information from each team member and they will present their project to the class. The project might be a bulletin board, model, display, oral presentation, skit, demonstrations, chart, student-made slides, or videos.

SUGGESTIONS FOR ACCOUNTABILITY:
- *Group:* Each team must create a group project.
- *Individual:* Each student must turn in a report on his/her mini-topic. A test could be given over the material.

> **Necessary Knowledge:** Students need to know how to use the library and how to write reports.
>
> **Cooperative Collaboration:** Each student on a team is responsible for teaching his/her mini-topic to the other members of the team.
>
> **Grand Finale:** A test or the group project could serve as the closure activity.

Next time I plan to _____

WILD ABOUT WILDFLOWERS

SUBJECT AREA: Science

GRADE LEVEL: 5-9

OBJECTIVES: Students will become familiar with wildflowers by learning their names, appearances, and characteristics.

MATERIALS:
- One wildflower guidebook per team
- One wildflower list per team
- One student instruction sheet per team
- Crayons or pastels
- Unlined white paper
- Encyclopedias
- One report folder per team

SUGGESTION FOR POSITIVE INTERDEPENDENCE:
The teacher will develop a list of about 36 wildflowers native to the region. Each team must choose 8 wildflowers to study. Wildflowers will be divided evenly among team members. Each team member will research his/her flower and will tell the other members of the team about that flower. Each student will have a specific job to help assemble the research report. There will be two illustrators, one calligrapher, and one compiler.

SUGGESTIONS FOR ACCOUNTABILITY:
- *Group:* 1. Each group must turn in a research project.
   2. Each team must share what they learned about their flowers with the other students in the class.
- *Individual:* 1. Each individual student will be assigned specific wildflowers to research.
   2. The teacher will also assign specific jobs to each team member. Two students will be illustrators, one student a calligrapher, and one a compiler.

WILD ABOUT WILDFLOWERS

Necessary Knowledge: Students need to know how to use the library to do research.

Cooperative Collaboration: Assign specific wildflowers to each team member. Each member is responsible for researching his/her wildflower and writing a report about it. When the research and reports are finished, students share their information with each other.
The two illustrators will draw pictures of the flowers that each team has researched.
The compiler will organize the reports and illustrations.

Grand Finale: Students will turn in the research folder for a grade. The teacher will call on different students to tell about certain wildflowers or to answer questions about wildflowers.

Wildflower List

_____ _____ _____ _____

_____ _____ _____ _____

_____ _____ _____ _____

_____ _____ _____ _____

_____ _____ _____ _____

_____ _____ _____ _____

_____ _____ _____ _____

_____ _____ _____ _____

WILD ABOUT WILDFLOWERS

Student Instruction Sheet

Step 1: Choose eight wildflowers from the wildflower list.

Step 2: Divide the wildflowers evenly among the students on your team.

Step 3: Each member of the team is responsible for researching his/her wildflowers and writing a one page report about the wildflower.

Step 4: After each team member has completed his/her report, the team needs to meet to proofread each other's reports.

Make corrections as needed. Don't forget to share with your team members any interesting information about your wildflower that may not be included in your report! Each team member is responsible for every other team member knowing about and being able to identify all the wildflowers on the list.

Step 5: Assign one of these jobs to each member of the team:
illustrator (assign two students to this role)
calligrapher
compiler

Members may want to volunteer for jobs they know they perform well or volunteer for jobs they want to learn how to do. Everyone must have a job!

A CREEPY ACTIVITY

SUBJECT AREA: Science

GRADE LEVEL: 5-9

OBJECTIVE:
- Students will research spiders.
- Students will investigate arachnophobia.

MATERIALS
- Paper
- Pencil
- Encyclopedia
- Reference books on spiders
- Dictionary
- All necessary work sheets

SUGGESTION FOR POSITIVE INTERDEPENDENCE:
After some initial independent research, the work sheet on "A Creepy Activity" should be completed together.

SUGGESTIONS FOR ACCOUNTABILITY:
- *Group:* Everyone must agree on the final work sheet that is turned in.
- *Individual:* Each student will research a specific aspect of "arachnophobia" and report his/her findings to the group.

Necessary Knowledge: None

Cooperative Collaboration: This project will be divided among the cooperative group; then a worksheet will be completed cooperatively.

Grand Finale:
- The students could watch the movie *Arachnophobia* or an old thriller movie that spotlighted spiders.
- The class could create a collection of spiders using actual spiders and pictures.

Next time I plan to _____

_____

A CREEPY ACTIVITY

I. Research

Choose a topic from the list of items below for an independent research project. After the topic is selected, research it thoroughly using your science book, encyclopedia, reference books, magazines, or newspapers. Write down as many facts as possible about the topic. You will share the information with the group.

Topics:
- phobia
- arachnophobia
- spiders (2 students could select this topic)
- entomologist
- characteristics of insects
- tarantulas

II. Discuss

Take about 10 minutes and share the information you learned about the topic with the group. Tell them the most important information you discovered.

III. Summarize

As a group, try to remember ten facts that were discussed about the topics. Summarize the facts into ten sentences and write them below.

1. _____
2. _____
3. _____
4. _____
5. _____
6. _____
7. _____
8. _____
9. _____
10. _____

Names _____

A CREEPY ACTIVITY

IV. Questions and Answers

From the research and the group discussion, answer the following questions.

1. Define "arachnophobia." _____

_____

2. Define phobia. _____

3. List at least three other common types of phobias. _____

_____

4. List four characteristics of a spider. _____

_____

5. Name three different types of spiders. _____

_____

6. What is an entomologist? _____

_____

7. If someone has a phobia, how can you tell? _____

_____

8. Name three things spiders like to eat. _____

_____

9. What is an exterminator? _____

_____

10. What are the differences between insects and spiders?_____

_____

V. Group Inventory

Arachnophobia was a movie released in the summer of 1990. The star of
the movie was Big Bob, a 9 inch long Amazon bird-eating tarantula.
Answer the questions below to determine if your group could have costared
with Big Bob.

1. How many of the group could pick up Big Bob? _____

2. How many of the group would not scream the first time they saw Big

   Bob?_____

3. How many in the group could let Big Bob walk up their leg? _____

4. How many in the group would have nightmares about Big Bob? ____

_____

Names _____

A CREEPY ACTIVITY

VI. Adjective Activity

As a group take five minutes and list as many adjectives as possible that could describe spiders.

_____

_____

_____

_____

_____

_____

VII. Conclusion

In the movie *Arachnophobia*, blow dryers were used to make the spiders move, and Lemon Pledge® furniture polish was the only substance used to make them stop. Let's suppose the classroom was infested with 30 Amazon bird-eating tarantulas. How would your group exterminate them? Write the group's plan below.

_____

_____

_____

_____

_____

_____

_____

Names _____

PARADE OF PLANETS

SUBJECT AREA: Science

GRADE LEVEL: 4-8

OBJECTIVE: Students will develop an understanding for the order of the planets from the sun and their size in relationship to each other.

MATERIALS:
- A large object that represents the sun for each group.
  Suggestions include: a large balloon, large circle cut from poster board, basketball, etc.
- 9 objects that could represent the 9 planets
  Suggestions include: a bean, head of lettuce, baseball, softball, orange, grapefruit, new potato, coins, button, a round piece of macaroni, a bottle cap, or round dry cereal
- A "Parade of Planets" work sheet
- Reference material on the planets
- Rulers

SUGGESTION FOR POSITIVE INTERDEPENDENCE:
The cooperative group will have nine objects per group to share. Each member of the group will have to help decide which objects represent which planets.

SUGGESTIONS FOR ACCOUNTABILITY:
- *Group:* The entire group must construct a Planet Parade to show to the entire class.
- *Individual:* Each group member will be responsible for discovering facts about each planet, in order for the group to know where to place the planet in the parade.

Necessary Knowledge: None

Cooperative Collaboration: Each group will produce a Planet Parade using the ten objects they are given. Students must practice the cooperative skill of giving further rationale for their answers.

Grand Finale: The Planet Parade could be used as a display in the classroom.

Next time I plan to _____

PARADE OF PLANETS

Step 1: Mercury, Venus, Earth, Mars, Jupiter, Saturn, Uranus, Neptune, and Pluto are planets in our solar system. First, cooperatively decide which group members will research which planets. For each planet the following facts must be found:

1. How far is the planet from the sun?
2. What is the planet's diameter? (Remember, the diameter is the distance all the way across the planet.)
3. What color does the planet appear to be, or what unusual characteristics does it have?

When the research has been completed, fill in the following fact sheet.

Planet Name _____   Planet Name _____
Distance from the sun _____   Distance from the sun _____
Color or characteristics _____   Color or characteristics _____

_____   _____
Diameter _____   Diameter _____

Planet Name _____   Planet Name _____
Distance from the sun _____   Distance from the sun _____
Color or characteristics _____   Color or characteristics _____

_____   _____
Diameter _____   Diameter _____

Planet Name _____   Planet Name _____
Distance from the sun _____   Distance from the sun _____
Color or characteristics _____   Color or characteristics _____

_____   _____
Diameter _____   Diameter _____

Planet Name _____   Planet Name _____
Distance from the sun _____   Distance from the sun _____
Color or characteristics _____   Color or characteristics _____

_____   _____
Diameter _____   Diameter _____

Planet Name _____
Distance from the sun _____
Color or characteristics _____

_____
Diameter _____

© 1991 by Incentive Publications, Inc., Nashville, TN
Names _____

PARADE OF PLANETS

Step 2: Using the research from step 1, determine which of the nine objects best represents each planet. Consider the size of each planet and its color or characteristics.

List below which object the cooperative group chose for each planet. Write a reason why that object was selected.

Planet named	Object selected	Why it was selected

Step 3: It is now time to organize the group's Planet Parade. Line up the objects that represent planets in the order they are found in our solar system. Write the order below, beginning at the sun and working outward.

Sun

_____

_____

_____

_____

_____

_____

_____

_____

_____

Step 4: Now actually line up the objects that represent the sun and the planets. When placing the objects, keep in mind that the distance from one planet to the next may not be consistent. Your group may want to estimate the differences, or the group may want to set up a type of scale using the ruler. (An example of a scale may be that 1 cm = 100,000,000 miles)

Step 5: Sketch your planet parade on the back of this sheet.

Names _____

WHAT CAUSES THE SEASONS?

SUBJECT AREA: Science

OBJECTIVE: Students will discover the sun gives off light and heat. The more sun rays that hit a section of the earth, the warmer that section will get.

MATERIALS:
- Two flashlights for each cooperative group
- Two thermometers for each cooperative group
- Black paper
- A globe
- Student instruction sheets

SUGGESTION FOR POSITIVE INTERDEPENDENCE:
Divide the cooperative groups into two groups of two students. Each two person group will be responsible for one of the flashlight activities. After the flashlight activities, each person on the team will explain to the other members what he/she discovered in the activity and how this knowledge can be used to explain the seasons we have on earth.

SUGGESTIONS FOR ACCOUNTABILITY:
- *Group:* The teacher will ask the spokesperson from each team to use a flashlight and globe to explain and demonstrate what causes the seasons.
- *Individual:* Each individual is responsible for a part of one of the flashlight activities explained on the student work sheet.

Necessary Knowledge: Students need to be able to read a thermometer. Students should know the earth is tilted on its axis.

Cooperative Collaboration: Students will have to be sure every member of the team understands that the angle of the sun's rays striking the surface of the earth causes the seasons. Students will not know which member will be called to explain it to the teacher. All students will receive their grade for this activity based on that one student's ability to explain the seasons.

Grand Finale:
1. The teacher will call on one member of the team to explain what causes the seasons. This person will also demonstrate it using a flashlight and a globe.
2. Team members will write a report telling what they think life would be like if the earth was not tilted on its axis.

Next time I plan to _____

WHAT CAUSES THE SEASONS?

Student Instruction Sheet

1. Shine a flashlight as shown in diagram 1.

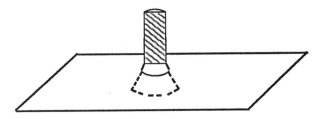

Diagram 1

What kind of area is covered by the light as it shines on the paper? _____
Trace this area on the paper. Now shine your flashlight on the same sheet of paper as shown in diagram 2.

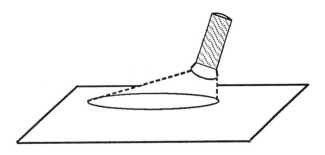

Diagram 2

Trace the area. What do you notice about the different areas? _____

_____
In which area, direct or slanted, do you think the temperature would be

greater? _____

2. Divide your cooperative learning team into two groups with two members in each group. Each group will need a flashlight, thermometer, a piece of black construction paper, and a chart for graphing its results.

Names _____

© 1991 by Incentive Publications, Inc., Nashville, TN

WHAT CAUSES THE SEASONS?

3. Group 1
Shine a flashlight as shown in diagram 1. Place a thermometer on the paper and record the results on the following chart.

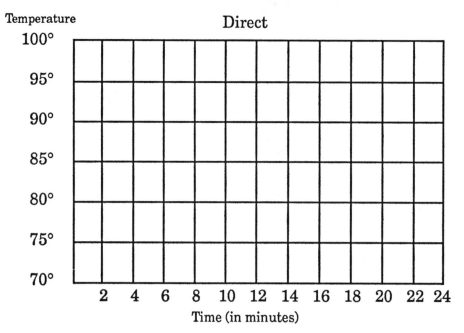

Group 2
Shine a flashlight as shown in diagram 2. Place a thermometer on the paper and record the results in the following chart.

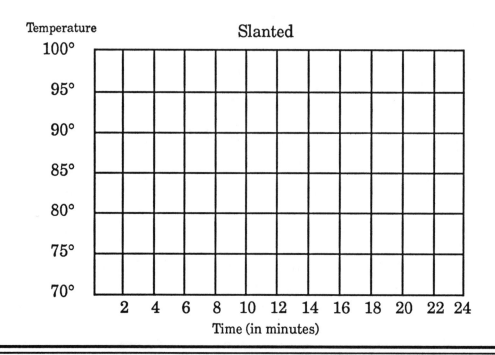

Names _____

WHAT CAUSES THE SEASONS?

4. Tell what you discovered about the difference in the temperature of the light when it is direct and when it is slanted.

_____

_____

_____

_____

_____

5. Use a globe and a flashlight to explain how the slant of the sun's rays causes the seasons.

6. As a group decide how you think life as we know it would be changed if the earth did not tilt on its axis. Tell what you think life would be like at the equator, in the northern hemisphere, southern hemisphere, and at the north and south poles.

_____

_____

_____

_____

_____

_____

*Answer Key

© 1991 by Incentive Publications, Inc., Nashville, TN

Names _____

Solar Roaster

SUBJECT AREA: Science

OBJECTIVES: The students will discover that the sun gives off heat and energy, and it is especially apparent when its rays are concentrated to one spot.

MATERIALS:
- Different sizes and shapes of bowls and boxes (Have lids available for some boxes.)
- Long forks or long pointed sticks, one for each team
- Sunglasses
- Sunscreen
- Student work sheet
- Aluminum foil
- Marshmallows

SUGGESTIONS FOR POSITIVE INTERDEPENDENCE:
All the students on a team must work together to design a solar cooker to be used to roast marshmallows.

SUGGESTIONS FOR ACCOUNTABILITY:
- *Group:* No one will be able to have a roasted marshmallow to eat unless all members work together to design and build the solar cooker.
- *Individual:* Assign each student a particular job: Aluminum foil person - lines the box or bowl with aluminum foil. Cooker - roasts the marshmallows. Timer - times how long it takes a marshmallow to roast in the cooker. Reporter - draws a picture of the marshmallow roaster that the team designed and reports on how long it took the marshmallows to roast.

Necessary Knowledge: Students need to know to never look directly at the sun. Students also need to know to never look directly at any glaring or bright spot on the solar cooker.
Always use the aluminum foil shiny side up. In order to find the best spot to roast the marshmallows, the student should hold his/her hand over the bowl or box and lower it until he/she finds the hot spot. Instruct them not to leave their hands there more than a few seconds.
Students need to wear sunscreen and sunglasses.

Cooperative Collaboration: All students will get to eat roasted marshmallows if they work together to successfully build a solar roaster.

Grand Finale:
1. Students will eat their roasted marshmallow.
2. The group with the design for the fastest marshmallow roaster will receive the golden marshmallow award.
3. Teams may want to try roasting hot dogs!

Next time I plan to _____

SOLAR ROASTER

Student Work Sheet

1. Choose a box or bowl to use to design a solar marshmallow roaster.

2. Assign each student a particular job.
   Aluminum Foil Person - lines the box or bowl with aluminum foil. (Don't forget - shiny side out!)
   Cooker - roasts the marshmallows
   Timer - times the cooker as he/she roasts each marshmallow and finds the average time to cook a marshmallow. (Remember, to find the average, you add all the times and divide by the number of times you added together.)
   Reporter - draws a picture of the solar cooker the team designed and reports the average time it took the team to roast a marshmallow.

3. Design and build your solar roaster. Remember, you are trying to use the aluminum foil to direct the sun's rays to a small "hot spot." This is the place where you will place your marshmallow to roast it.

4. Actually roast your marshmallows. Don't forget to record the time every time you roast a marshmallow. Yes, you may cooperatively share the marshmallows after you roast them.

5. Fill out the team report form.

Team Report Form

_____ Aluminum Foil Person

_____ Cooker

_____ Timer

_____ Reporter

Include an illustration of the solar cooker you designed.

Average time to roast a marshmallow using this cooker. _____

Names _____

BLUEPRINT FOR SOCIAL STUDIES

SUBJECT AREA: Social Studies

GRADE LEVEL: 4-9

OBJECTIVE: Using the cooperative learning method, the teacher will devise new techniques for teaching social studies.

MATERIALS:
- Paper
- Pencil
- Text
- Reference materials

SUGGESTIONS FOR POSITIVE INTERDEPENDENCE:
- **Group Reports -** A cooperative group is assigned a specific topic. Each member is responsible for researching one source and reporting back to the group. The group would then assemble all the resources into a final report.
- **Reading Pairs -** A cooperative group of two is established. One student reads a paragraph from the text or resource material. Then the second student summarizes that paragraph orally to his/her partner. Then the second student reads the next paragraph, and the first student summarizes it.
- **Think and Do Groups -** A set of questions is assigned to a group. The group thinks how they want to divide the task; then they do their questions. The group must remember that only one paper will be turned in for a grade.
- **Cut and Paste -** A group of questions is assigned – all the students do the assignment. Then they reassemble and choose the best answers from all the papers. At this point, those answers are cut out of the students' papers and pasted on one final sheet to turn in. (Remember to instruct the students to write only on one side of their paper.)
- **Quiz Quest -** Each cooperative group makes up a quiz over the current subject. Then the groups swap the quizzes and answer them. Then another cooperative group checks the quizzes!

BLUEPRINT FOR SOCIAL STUDIES

SUGGESTIONS FOR ACCOUNTABILITY:
- *Group:* The teacher should be monitoring all groups to ensure a good delegation of responsibility among the groups. Verbal praise or tokens could be given for following cooperative norms of behavior.
- *Individual:* During some of the activities, it would be appropriate to let the groups meet one day and assign specific tasks to do as cooperative homework. The following day the group meets and organizes the assignments.

Necessary Knowledge: Students need to have an introduction to cooperative behavior.

Cooperative Collaboration: When the teacher monitors the groups, he/she should give verbal praise or tokens to the group following cooperative norms of behavior.

Grand Finale: Depending on the specific group activity, different closure activities would be appropriate.

Some suggestions are as follows:
- A group processing inventory
- Class discussion
- Formal assessment
- Oral reports
- Written reports
- A similar follow-up assignment

Next time I plan to _____

_____

PACES TO PLACES

SUBJECT AREA: Math or social studies

GRADE LEVEL: 4-8

SKILL:
- Measuring with a ruler
- Determining distance in miles

OBJECTIVES: The students will determine how long it will take them to walk specific distances.

MATERIALS:
- Ruler
- "Paces to Places" work sheets
- Calculator (recommended but not required)
- An atlas or a map with a scale
- A watch, stopwatch, or clock

SUGGESTION FOR POSITIVE INTERDEPENDENCE:
Students will have to aid each other when they measure the paces.

SUGGESTIONS FOR ACCOUNTABILITY: All students will have to complete a "Paces to Places" work sheet using their own pace measurements.

Necessary Knowledge:
- How to measure with a ruler to the nearest inch
- Students must know that 1 mile = 5,280 feet

Cooperative Collaboration: The lesson involves several different "jobs" (measuring, calculating, filling out the work sheets). These jobs should be distributed among all group members.

Grand Finale: "Paces to Places" is a lesson that should be followed up with a group processing activity.

Next time I plan to _____

_____

PACES TO PLACES

All group members need to determine the length of their pace. A pace is the distance traveled when someone takes two normal steps. The way to measure a pace is to measure the distance from the tip of your right shoe in the first step to the tip of the right shoe in the second step (see diagram).

Step 1: Write the distance of each student's pace in the chart below. It will take some cooperation to measure a pace. (One person can't do it alone.)

Name	Length of pace (to the nearest inch)

Describe how the group cooperated to measure a pace. _____

_____

_____

Step 2: Each group member should walk the length and width of the classroom and record how many paces it took him/her.

Name	Length (paces)	Width (paces)

Names _____

PACES TO PLACES

Step 3: Each member converts the paces in the chart for step 2 to inches and fills in the chart below. Use only the measurements you have on the charts.

Write down the method you will use to do this conversion. _____

_____

Name	Length of classroom (inch)	Width of classroom (inch)

Did the measurement of the length and width of the room come out the same no matter who measured it? _____

If the measurement of the length and width of the room did not come out the same, how can the group explain the difference? _____

_____

Step 4: There are 5,280 feet in a mile. How many inches are in a mile? (This is a good time to use a calculator if you have one!) _____

Names _____

PACES TO PLACES

Step 5: Using the information in steps 1 and 4, complete the chart below.

Name	Pace length	How many paces would make a mile?

Step 6: Using a map or an atlas, determine the distance from one place to another. Then determine how many paces it would take each of you to walk to the destination.

Distance from _____ to _____ is _____ miles.

Name	Number of paces to destination

Names _____

More...Paces to Places

Step 1 Enrichment:

Find an area where an 18 yard line can be measured off. (This is slightly more than 1/100 of a mile). Each group member should walk that 18 yards at a normal pace. Fill out the chart below.

Name	Time to walk 18 yards (1/100 of a mile)

Step 2 Enrichment:

Using the data from step 1 enrichment, determine how long it would take each group member to walk one mile at a normal pace. How will you determine this? Write your method below.

Name	Time to walk one mile

Names _____

More...Paces to Places

Step 3 Enrichment:

Using a map, determine a distance from one place to another. How long would it take each student to walk that distance?

Distance from _____ to _____ in

miles is _____ .

Fill in the chart below.

Name	Time to walk to destination

Super Enrichment:

Determine how many miles per hour each group member is walking.

Name	Miles per hour

Names _____

HAPPY TRAILS TO YOU!

SUBJECT AREA: Social Studies

GRADE LEVEL: 5-9

SKILL:
- Drawing a map
- Giving directions

MATERIALS:
- Rulers
- Paper
- Pencils
- City map
- "Happy Trails" work sheet

SUGGESTION FOR POSITIVE INTERDEPENDENCE:
Different members of the cooperative group will know where different points of interest can be located. The cooperative group will have to function as a group to locate all items on the list.

SUGGESTIONS FOR ACCOUNTABILITY:
- *Group:* The group members must check each other's map for accuracy. The group members' maps could be graded individually; then the group grade could be an average of all individual grades.
- *Individual:* Each group member must complete a map on his/her own.

Necessary Knowledge: None

Cooperative Collaboration: The teacher should observe all groups to ensure that all members are participating in the activity. This should be done using a teacher's observation checklist.

Grand Finale: If all the locations are within walking distance, a field trip could be planned to walk to all the different locations. The field trip could be set up as a scavenger hunt. The groups could go to each location and pick up some type of token. Volunteers would be necessary to supervise the groups and hand out tokens. The first group to return to the starting point would be the winners of the hunt.

Students could use a city map to map out their route to the locations and measure the actual distance of the route. Then the cooperative groups could discover which group found the shortest route.

This cooperative activity could serve as an introduction to other map skills taught in the social studies curriculum.

Next time I plan to _____

Happy Trails to You!

The purpose of this activity is to discover how well the group knows the neighborhood around the school. Each group member will draw a map that will show how to get to each location. The first objective of this activity is to draw an accurate map. Next, draw the shortest route to the specific location. (Try not to backtrack if possible.) If there are several locations in the neighborhood where the places can be found, decide **cooperatively** which location is the most convenient. Begin your map by placing yourself at the front door of the school. Happy trails to you!

Step 1: As a group, decide where the following items are located. Do not include locations within your school building. All locations must be out of the school.

Items/places to locate	The nearest location is:
Newspaper Stand	_____
Soft Drink Machine	_____
Elementary School	_____
Bank	_____
Public Telephone	_____
Public Library	_____
Gas Station	_____
Fast Food Restaurant	_____

Step 2: Each group member must now draw a map showing each location listed. Make your maps clear, accurate, and neat.

Step 3: Trade maps with others in the group. Can the map be read easily? If not, correct any errors.

ENRICHMENT:
- Draw a map of the neighborhood where you live. Label important landmarks around your neighborhood.
- A long lost relative just arrived at the school office. This long lost relative needs to go from the school to your home. Write clear directions to your home.

Names _____

Martin & Me

SUBJECT AREA: Social Studies

GRADE LEVEL: 5-9

OBJECTIVE: Students will learn more about Dr. Martin Luther King, Jr., and will present the information to the class by making and illustrating a group timeline.

MATERIALS:
- Reference materials from the library
- Long strips of paper for each team
- Felt-tip markers
- Textbook
- "Martin & Me" instruction sheet

SUGGESTIONS FOR POSITIVE INTERDEPENDENCE:
1. Divide Martin Luther King's life into enough equal parts so each member of the team has a small section of his life to research for the timeline.
2. Each team is given four different colored markers. After the students have researched Dr. King's life, each will use a different color marker to label and illustrate a timeline about Dr. King's life.

SUGGESTIONS FOR ACCOUNTABILITY:
- *Group:* Each group will complete a timeline.
- *Individual:* Each individual is responsible for researching a period of Dr. King's life. Each individual is also responsible for drawing that period of Dr. King's life onto the team timeline.

Necessary Knowledge:
1. Students will need to understand the concept of timelines.
2. Students need to know how to use reference materials in a library.

Cooperative Collaboration:
1. Students will complete a timeline about Dr. Martin Luther King, Jr. Each student will be responsible for certain years of Dr. King's life, and each team member must do his/her own research in order to complete the project on time.
2. Students will also have to decide on individual responsibilities when they actually draw their team's timelines.

Grand Finale: Each team will have a representative present its timeline and one very interesting fact the team learned about Dr. King to the rest of the class.

Teacher's Note: This activity may be used to study any historical figure.

Next time I plan to _____

MARTIN & ME

Student Instruction Sheet

1. Dr. Martin Luther King, Jr., lived from 1929-1968. Divide his life into sections so each member of your team will have a part of his life to research. Since there will probably be more information about his life from college years to his death than about his early life, you may not want to divide it evenly.

2. Assign specific years of Dr. King's life to each team member.

3. Each member of the team must individually research Dr. King's life to find information about the important events during his/her assigned years.

4. When each member of the team has completed his/her research, share the facts about Dr. King's life with each other.

5. Plan how you will put this information on a four-color timeline. Each student will be assigned one color marker, and he/she may use only that color.

DIFFERENT STROKES FOR DIFFERENT FOLKS

SUBJECT AREA: Social Studies

GRADE LEVEL: 5-9

OBJECTIVE: The students will learn about some of the different cultures of the world, build a model of what housing would have been like in that culture, and share information about the culture with other class members.

MATERIALS:
- Reference materials from the library
- Social studies textbook
- One large piece of sturdy, corrugated cardboard per team
- Glue
- Clay
- Sugar cubes
- Aluminum foil
- Fake fur or imitation animal skins material
- String
- Small sticks and twigs
- Student instruction sheet

SUGGESTIONS FOR POSITIVE INTERDEPENDENCE:
1. Assign a different culture to each cooperative learning group.
2. Each member of the team should research the culture to determine why and what type of housing that group of people used, their occupations, and what the climate was like where they lived. Each team member should have a different topic to research about his/her culture.
3. After all the students have completed their research, they should get together and share the information with each other.
4. Finally, the team will design and build a replica of what the culture they studied was like and present it to the rest of the class.

SUGGESTIONS FOR ACCOUNTABILITY:
- *Group:* Each group will complete a replica of the housing of the culture they studied.
- *Individual:* When the group presents its model to the rest of the class, each member of the group must tell what he/she has learned about this culture through his/her research.

Necessary Knowledge: Students need to know how to use reference materials in a library.

Cooperative Collaboration: The students will complete a replica of the housing of the culture they studied.

Grand Finale: Each team will present its replica to the rest of the class. Individual team members will tell the class what they learned when they researched their culture.

Next time I plan to _____

98

DIFFERENT STROKES FOR DIFFERENT FOLKS

Before the groups begin their research, assign the different cultures to the different teams.
One way you could do this is to let each team randomly draw slips of paper with the name of a different culture on each piece of paper. You may also want to allow each team to choose a culture they are interested in researching, or you may simply want to assign topics.

Some possible topics are listed below. Choose the topics that will best fit with your curriculum:

Inca

Aborigines

Hebrews

Lapps

Japanese

Chinese

Eskimo

Iroquois Indians

Sioux Indians

Cherokee Indians

Navaho Indians

Hawaiians

DIFFERENT STROKES FOR DIFFERENT FOLKS

Student Instruction Sheet

1. Your teacher has just assigned a specific culture to your cooperative learning group. Each member of this group is responsible for going to the library and researching this particular culture.

2. The **Runner** needs to research to find out what the housing looks/looked like in this culture.

   The **Checker** needs to research to find out why this culture uses/used this particular type of housing.

   The **Reporter** needs to research to find out whether or not the people in this culture are/were hunters, farmers, or fishers. Do these people stay in the same place or are they nomadic?

   The **Encourager** needs to research to find out about the climate.

3. After each team member has completed his/her research, the team needs to share all the information with each other.

4. The team needs to decide how they can build a model of a house that is representative of their culture. Spend several days building your model on a large piece of cardboard.

5. When all the teams have completed their replicas, the teams will be called on to present the model to the rest of the class and to orally share the information discovered about this culture during research. Remember, every member of the group will have to share during this oral presentation.

AMUSEMENT LAND

SUBJECT AREA: Mathematics

GRADE LEVEL: 5-8

SKILL: Students will use various consumer math skills while planning a visit to an amusement park.

OBJECTIVES:
- Students will write ratios.
- Students will determine how to spend $10 on lunch and souvenirs.
- Students will determine sales tax.
- Students will determine the cost per ride at an amusement park.

MATERIALS:
- "Amusement Land" problem card
- "Amusement Land" role-playing cards
- "Amusement Land" ride sheet
- "Amusement Land" souvenir price sheet
- "Amusement Land" student answer sheet

SUGGESTION FOR POSITIVE INTERDEPENDENCE:
All group members must help each other answer the student answer sheet.

SUGGESTIONS FOR ACCOUNTABILITY:
- *Group:* The group must reach a consensus on the six rides they will ride at the amusement park.
- *Individual:* Each student is assigned a different role and must solve the problem on that particular role-playing card.

Necessary Knowledge: Students need to be able to add whole numbers. Students should be able to write ratios in simplest form. Students need to be able to multiply mixed numbers. Students should be able to divide with a decimal in the dividends place.

Cooperative Collaboration: The students must read the problem card together and decide which students will be assigned each role. Then the group must cooperatively decide which six rides they will ride together.

Grand Finale: The students will complete the student work sheet. The class could plan a field trip to a local amusement park.

Next time I plan to _____

AMUSEMENT LAND

AMUSEMENT LAND PROBLEM CARD

1. Suppose you and your friends are going to the amusement park. Using the "Ride Sheet," choose six rides. Add the time of the ride and the time you must wait in line to determine the total time for all six rides.

2. From the information on the "Ride Sheet," write a ratio comparing the time on each ride you selected to the time you must spend in line. Then write a ratio comparing the total time on the rides you selected to the total time you must wait in line. Reduce this ratio; write in fractional form if possible.

3. You have $10 each to spend on souvenirs and lunch. Use the menu and the souvenir price sheet in the station box to determine what each of you buys with your money. Remember to include sales tax.

4. If there are 14 rides at this amusement park and you paid $19.95 for admission, what is the cost per ride?

Names _____

AMUSEMENT LAND

AMUSEMENT LAND ROLE-PLAYING CARDS

Character 1: *Time Monitor*
With the other students, choose six mutually agreeable rides. Then using the "Ride Sheet," add the times.

Character 2: *Ratio Writer*
Write the ratio of the time on the ride to the time in the line for both individual rides and the total of rides. You will need to use the "Ride Sheet."

Example:

Ride	Time on Ride	Time in Line
Corkscrew	15 min.	40 min.
Ratio of time on ride to time in line		15/40 or 3/8

Character 3: *Money Manager*
Ask the other team members what they plan to eat and what souvenirs they plan to buy. Total the prices and add sales tax. Be sure no one spends more than $10 including the sales tax.

Example:

If your subtotal is $7.43 and you need to find out how much tax you owe, you multiply 7.43 x sales tax = _____   (Example: 7.43 x .0775 = _____)

If you are using a calculator, you multiply 7.43 x sales tax = _____
(Example: 7.43 x 7.75% = _____)

Character 4: *Price Fixer*
The admission fee is $19.95. If there are 14 rides at this amusement park and you plan to ride all of them, what is the cost per ride?

© 1991 by Incentive Publications, Inc., Nashville, TN

Names _____

AMUSEMENT LAND

AMUSEMENT LAND RIDE SHEET

Rides	Time on Ride	Time in Line
Tube Roller	5 min.	10 min.
Log Lunge	6 min.	5 min.
Sky Ride	8 min.	6 min.
Railroad	15 min.	20 min.
Auto Freeway	8 min.	10 min.
The Big Splash	6 min.	15 min.
Loop the Loop	5 min.	15 min.
Swingtime	4 min.	8 min.
Bumper Cars	4 min.	10 min.
White Water Rafting	9 min.	30 min.
Roller Coaster	4 min.	10 min.
Swirl Around	5 min.	7 min.
3-D Scream	6 min.	30 min.

AMUSEMENT LAND

AMUSEMENT LAND MENU

Hamburger $2.00
Hot Dog..1.50
French Fries .... .60
Taco.. .79
Salad..2.00
Fried Chicken..2.00
Fried Fish..2.00
Cole Slaw... .65
Mashed Potatoes... .55
Ice Cream .... .75
Funnel Cake .... .80
Popcorn .... .50
Nachos 1.00
Soft Drinks .... .80
Milk.. .50
Fruit Drink.. .75

AMUSEMENT LAND SOUVENIRS

Hat...$4.00
T-shirt 5.00
Postcard .... .25
Key Ring 1.00
Mug..2.00
Stuffed Animal 6.00
Poster...2.00
Map..1.00
Photo..2.50

AMUSEMENT LAND
ANSWER SHEET

1. List your six rides, the time for each ride, and the total time on the rides.

   Name of the ride   **Time on the ride**

   _____   _____
   _____   _____
   _____   _____
   _____   _____
   _____   _____
   _____   _____

                     Total time on rides _____

2. List your six rides, the ratios of the time on the ride to the time in the line, and the ratio of the total time on the rides to the total time in the lines.

   Name of the ride   **Ratio**

   _____   _____
   _____   _____
   _____   _____
   _____   _____
   _____   _____

   Ratio of total time in lines to total time on rides _____

3. List what each student plans to spend for food and for souvenirs, total the prices, and add the sales tax.

   Student 1   **Student 2**

   _____   _____
   _____   _____
   _____   _____
   _____   _____
   _____   _____

   Subtotal _____   Subtotal _____
   Tax   _____   Tax   _____
   Total   _____   Total   _____

   Student 3   **Student 4**

   _____   _____
   _____   _____
   _____   _____
   _____   _____
   _____   _____

   Subtotal _____   Subtotal _____
   Tax   _____   Tax   _____
   Total   _____   Total   _____

Names _____

MUSIC MADNESS

SUBJECT AREA: Mathematics

GRADE LEVEL: 5-8

SKILL: Students will practice various consumer math skills while deciding how to purchase concert tickets to get the best value for their money.

OBJECTIVES:
- Students will add and subtract whole numbers.
- Students will multiply and divide mixed numbers.
- Students will multiply with decimals.
- Students will find the percent of a number.

MATERIALS:
- "Music Madness" problem card
- "Music Madness" role-playing cards
- "Music Madness" concert schedule
- "Music Madness" student answer sheet

SUGGESTIONS FOR POSITIVE INTERDEPENDENCE: All group members must contribute answers on the student answer sheet.

SUGGESTIONS FOR ACCOUNTABILITY:
- *Group:* The group must reach a consensus on which concerts they will attend together and the best way to purchase the tickets.
- *Individual:* Each student is assigned a different role and must solve the problem on the particular role-playing card.

Necessary Knowledge: Students need to be able to add and subtract whole numbers. Students should be able to multiply and divide mixed numbers. Students need to be able to multiply decimals. Students should be able to find the percent of a number.

Cooperative Collaboration: The students must read the problem card together and decide which students will be assigned each role. The students must decide which of the concerts they will attend together.

Grand Finale: The students will complete the student work sheet. The students could be allowed to bring in their favorite musical tape or CD for the class to listen to on the last day of the class.

Next time I plan to _____

Music Madness

MUSIC MADNESS PROBLEM CARD

1. You and your friends each have $55 to spend on concerts this summer. Using the concert schedule sheet, decide which concerts you all want to see.

2. The Temptations and the Four Tops will perform together. Given the length of time they will perform and the playing length of their average song, which group will perform the most songs?

3. If you make minimum wage at a local fast food restaurant, how many hours will you have to work in order to purchase tickets to the concerts you want to attend?

4. Compare different ticket prices to determine the best financial deal.

Names _____

Music Madness

MUSIC MADNESS STUDENT ROLE-PLAYING CARDS

Character 1: *Ticket Agent*

You and your friends each have $55 to spend on concerts this summer. Using the concert sheet, try to schedule a variety of concerts so all members of your group are satisfied. You will also need to decide if you want to purchase reserved seat tickets or general admission tickets.
You need to save enough money from your $55 to pay for parking. It costs $3 each time you go to the music area.

cut here

Character 2: *Song Counter*

The Temptations and the Four Tops will perform together on October 19. The average length of a song by the Temptations is 4 ½ minutes. The average length of a song by the Four Tops is 3 ¾ minutes. The Temptations will perform for 1 hour and the Four Tops will perform for 1 ½ hours. Which group will sing the most songs? How many more?

cut here

MUSIC MADNESS

MUSIC MADNESS STUDENT ROLE-PLAYING CARDS

Character 3: *Wage Earner*

You make minimum wage working at a local fast food restaurant. You work 20 hours per week. Ten percent of your weekly check is deducted for taxes. How many weeks will you have to work to buy reserved seat tickets to see Elton John on May 9, Aerosmith on May 18, Don Henley on June 1, Janet Jackson on July 8, Robert Plant on July 29, and New Kids on the Block on August 16? How long would you have to work if you were going to buy two reserved seat tickets to each of the concerts so you could take a friend?

cut here

Character 4: *Bargain Hunter*

A Music Club Card entitles you to two general admission tickets for any ten concerts. The Music Club Card costs $125. Should you buy the Music Club Card or purchase ten individual general admission tickets? How much money would you save?

(Don't forget that the Music Club Card entitles you to two general admission tickets per concert!)

cut here

Music Madness

CONCERT SCHEDULE

May		Res.	Gen.
9	Elton John	$18.50	$15.50
18	Aerosmith	19.50	17.50
26	Hank Williams Jr.	19.50	16.50

June			
1	Don Henley	19.50	17.50
16	The Temptations / The Four Tops	18.00	15.50
18	Chuck Mangione	18.00	15.50
19	Crosby, Stills, and Nash	18.50	16.00
20	Ray Charles	19.50	17.50
29	Heart	19.50	17.50

July			
3	The B-52's	18.50	16.00
8	Janet Jackson	22.00	20.00
13	The Grateful Dead	19.00	17.00
19	Steve Miller	19.00	16.50
22	Phil Collins	23.00	20.00
29	Robert Plant	22.00	20.00

August			
7	George Strait / Patty Loveless	18.00	16.00
16	New Kids On The Block	24.00	21.00
18	Dolly Parton / Ricky Van Shelton / Doug Stone	22.00	20.00
21	Eric Clapton	22.00	20.00
25	The Rolling Stones	24.00	21.00

MUSIC MADNESS

Character 1

Concerts		Ticket Cost
_____		_____
_____		_____
_____		_____
_____		_____
_____		_____
_____		_____

Total parking costs   _____

Total cost   _____

(Did you have any money left? How much?)   _____

Character 2

How many songs will the Temptations sing? _____

How many songs will the Four Tops sing?   _____

Which group will sing the most songs?   _____

How many more songs?   _____

Example for how to divide mixed numbers:

$$2 \frac{1}{2} \div 1 \frac{1}{3} =$$
$$\frac{5}{2} \div \frac{4}{3} =$$
$$\frac{5}{2} \times \frac{3}{4} = \frac{15}{8} = 1 \frac{7}{8}$$

Names _____

Music Madness

Character 3

How much do you earn per week? _____

How much will you pay in taxes? _____

Subtract these numbers
(This is your take-home pay.) _____

How much money do you have to spend? _____

List ticket prices

_____

_____

_____

_____

_____

_____

Total costs _____

How long would you have to work to buy one
reserved seat ticket to each concert? _____

How long would you have to work to buy two
reserved seat tickets? _____

Character 4

What is the average price of a general admission ticket? _____

What would be the average price of ten general admission tickets? _____

Should you buy the Music Club Card or individual tickets?

_____

How much money would you save? _____

MCSOVIET

SUBJECT AREA: Mathematics

GRADE LEVEL: 5-8

SKILL: The students will count, play rubles, average numbers, and solve percent problems.

OBJECTIVES:
- The students will determine what percentage of the average wage would be spent at McDonald's® on a meal.
- The students will develop an understanding of the capacity of the McDonald's® restaurant in the Soviet Union.

MATERIALS:
- "McSoviet" problem card
- "McSoviet" role-playing card
- "McSoviet" helpful hint sheet
- "McSoviet" work sheet
- Pencil
- Paper

SUGGESTION FOR POSITIVE INTERDEPENDENCE:
The students will be assigned roles during the problem-solving activity.

SUGGESTIONS FOR ACCOUNTABILITY:
- *Group:* The students will receive a grade on the "McSoviet" work sheet.
- *Individual:* The students will have specific roles to perform during the lesson.

Necessary Knowledge:
- The students must have the math skills of an average fifth grader.
- The students should have some previous instruction with percentage problems.

Cooperative Collaboration:
- Students must read the cards included in the problem-solving boxes together.
- The students must decide cooperatively which roles to assign to the group members.

Next time I plan to _____

_____

McSoviet

Grand Finale:
- The students will do the "McSoviet" work sheet.
- An interdisciplinary activity could be done so students could study about the Soviet Union in social studies and in language arts class.
- The students could write to McDonald's® and learn more about the Soviet McDonald's®. The address is:

  McDonald's® Restaurants of Canada Limited
  McDonald's® Place
  Toronto, Ontario
  M3C 3L4

Teacher's Note: Play rubles are not included in this learning package. The teacher can make coins to represent rubles. Sketched below are three possible coins. Inform the class that these are not copies of actual rubles. The teacher should have a total of 18 rubles to represent the average Soviet wage.

McSoviet

The grand opening of the Moscow McDonald's® was on January 31, 1990. The new restaurant is located on Gorky Street and Pushkin Square within walking distance of the Kremlin. It is a state-of-the-art facility and is the largest McDonald's® restaurant in the world. Over 28,000 customers were served the first day in the 700 seat restaurant. The cost of the Big Mak (Big Mac®), Kartofel (fries), and a Koktel (Coke®) is 5.60 rubles. In the problem-solving package is the amount of rubles an average Soviet worker makes in one day. (See the package for information on how to calculate this figure.) The following questions must be answered in order to complete this activity:

- What is the average Soviet wage per day?
- What is the percentage of the cost of a Big Mak, Kartofel, and Koktel to the average daily wage?
- Does the average worker make enough in one day to feed a family of four at McDonald's®? Why or why not?
- How many times would the restaurant have to be filled in order to serve the record crowd on the first day?

ROLE-PLAYING CARD

Character 1: This character should count the money and determine how many rubles the average Soviet worker makes in one day.

cut here

Character 2: This character determines the percentage of the cost of a Big Mak, Kartofel, and Koktel to the average daily wage.

cut here

McSoviet

Character 3: This character determines if the average worker makes enough in one day to feed a family of four. This character must present the answer to the group and write the explanation on the work sheet.

cut here

Character 4:

This character will decide how many times the restaurant had to be filled in order to serve the record crowd on opening day.

cut here

HELPFUL HINT

How to find what percent one number is to another number.

Example : $\dfrac{\text{Cost of the meal}}{\text{Wages}} = \dfrac{?}{100}$

Names _____

McSoviet

STUDENT WORK SHEET

1. List the name of each group member and the character he/she was assigned.

   Character 1 _____

   Character 2 _____

   Character 3 _____

   Character 4 _____

2. What is the average Soviet wage for one day? _____

3. What percentage of this wage does a meal at McDonald's® cost? _____

4. Does the average worker make enough in one day to feed a family of four? _____ Explain your answer, and list what was purchased for the family. _____

   _____

5. How many times would the restaurant have to be filled in order to serve the record crowd on opening day? _____

*Answer Key

Names _____

Party On! Pizza Party

SUBJECT AREA: Mathematics

GRADE LEVEL: 5-8

SKILL: Various consumer math skills will be used in ordering a pizza.

OBJECTIVES:
- The students will evaluate various coupons dealing with ordering a pizza.
- The students will solve percentage problems.

MATERIALS:
- "Party On! Pizza Party" problem card
- "Party On! Pizza Party" role-playing card
- "Party On! Pizza Party" helpful hints sheet
- "Party On! Pizza Party" work sheet
- Calculator (optional)
- Pencil
- Paper

SUGGESTION FOR POSITIVE INTERDEPENDENCE:
All group members will have input concerning the type of pizza they want to order.

SUGGESTIONS FOR ACCOUNTABILITY:
- *Group:* The group must reach a consensus on the type of pizzas ordered.
- *Individual:* All members must help complete the "Party On! Pizza Party" work sheet.

PARTY ON! PIZZA PARTY

Necessary Knowledge:
- The students must be able to do basic math operations.
- The students should have some exposure to percentage-type problems.

Cooperative Collaboration: The students must read the problem card together and assume different roles for this activity.

Grand Finale:
- The students will complete the "Party On! Pizza Party" work sheet.
- An actual pizza party could be planned for the class.

Teacher's Notes:
A realistic feel can be added to this lesson by collecting actual pizza coupons and placing them in the problem-solving box. If the teacher is unable to secure coupons, a mock pizza parlor sheet for Mama's Pizzeria is provided.

Most any large pizza chain will supply you with a price list. If several price lists were included in this lesson, activities on price comparisons could be developed.

Next time I plan to _____

_____

PARTY ON! PIZZA PARTY

PROBLEM CARD

This Friday night you are having the cooperative group over to your house for a pizza. You can order from any pizza place you choose. The following questions must be answered in order to have a successful pizza party:

- How many and what size pizzas need to be ordered?

- What does everyone want on their pizza?

- From whom should you order the pizza?

- Are you going to use a coupon? Why or why not?

- What is the total bill for the pizzas?

- What will you tip the pizza driver?

- If the sales tax is 6 percent, how much tax will be on the order?

ROLE-PLAYING CARD

Character 1: You must help the group decide what type of pizzas to order.

Character 2: You must decide how many and what size pizzas to order.

Character 3: You are the manager of the pizza parlor. You must total the pizza order. (Don't forget the tax!)

Character 4: You are the party assistant. Figure the tip for the driver.

PARTY ON! PIZZA PARTY

HELPFUL HINTS

Hint 1: Notice how much toppings cost if ordered separately. Be sure to include all extra toppings starting with the basic cheese pizza price.

Hint 2: To figure the sales tax, take the total for the pizzas and multiply it by 6 percent.

There are two ways to do this.

> **Method One** - Using a calculator, take the total of the pizza, multiply by 6, and hit the percent key.
>
> - Example: 12.97 x 6% = .77

The total price including tax is 12.97 + .77 = 13.74

> **Method Two** - Change 6% to a decimal .06 and multiply by the total.
>
> - Example: 12.97 x .06 = .77

The total bill is 12.97 + .77 = 13.74

Hint 3: To determine the tip for the delivery person, multiply the total by 15 percent or by what the standard tip percentage is.

PARTY ON! PIZZA PARTY

Mama's Pizzeria

Type of Pizzas	12"	16"
Mama's Favorite	11.24	15.57

(pepperoni, sausage, onions, green peppers, extra
cheese, mushrooms, black olives, ham, ground beef)

Papa's Favorite	10.28	14.18

(pepperoni, sausage, onions, and extra cheese)

Little Tony's Favorite	9.98	11.28

(pepperoni, bacon, and ham)

Vegetarian Vennie's Favorite	9.99	11.98

(Green peppers, onions, fresh mushrooms,
green olives, and double cheese)

Basic Cheese Pizza	6.44	8.62

Other Choices

Choose from Mama's toppings:

Pepperoni	.96 each	1.39 each
Sausage		
Ham		
Ground Beef		
Double Cheese		
Fresh Mushrooms		
Green Peppers		
Onions		
Green Olives		
Black Olives		
Hot Pepper Rings		
Anchovies		
16 oz. drinks		.99 each

PARTY ON! PIZZA PARTY

COUPONS

Double Dare $12.95

Order two 16" cheese pizzas (tax not included).
Each additional topping just $1.95, covers both pizzas.

$12.95
(Tax not included.)

Large 3 Toppings $10.99

Order one large 16" cheese pizza with 3 toppings and pay

$10.99
(Tax not included.)

Party Discount
We Cater!

Let us cater your next party. Order 1-5 pizzas

and get a **10%** discount.

FREE

Six-pack of cola

with any Large Mama's Favorite(s)

PARTY ON! PIZZA PARTY

STUDENT WORK SHEET

1. Complete the chart below:

Quantity	Size of pizza	Ingredients on pizza	Price

2. Where will you order the pizzas from? _____

   Why was this restaurant selected? _____

3. Will you use a coupon?_____ If so, which coupon and why?

   _____

   _____

4. Including tax, what is the total bill for the pizza? _____

5. What will the driver's tip be? _____

6. All together, including tip and tax, what was the cost of the pizza party?

   _____

7. What was the average cost per person for pizza? _____

Names _____

EVERY DAY IS EARTH DAY

SUBJECT AREA: Mathematics or science

GRADE LEVEL: 5-8

SKILL: Using ecological information, students will solve problems that will create an environmental awareness.

OBJECTIVES:
- The students will become more ecologically-minded.
- The students will use addition, subtraction, multiplication, and division to solve story problems.
- The students will use basic percent principles.

MATERIALS:
- "Every Day is Earth Day" problem-solving card
- "Every Day is Earth Day" role-playing card
- "Every Day is Earth Day" helpful hints sheet
- "Every Day is Earth Day" student work sheet
- "Every Day is Earth Day" follow-up student work sheet
- Paper
- Pencil
- Calculator (optional)

EVERY DAY IS EARTH DAY

SUGGESTION FOR POSITIVE INTERDEPENDENCE:
The students will work together to solve problems dealing with environmental issues. Not only will the students use the cooperative model in the classroom, but this lesson will promote the idea that care of the environment is a cooperative community effort.

SUGGESTIONS FOR ACCOUNTABILITY:
- *Group:* The group will agree on the answers on the work sheet and will have to collaborate on the environmental question.
- *Individual:* The students will have a specific aspect of the work sheet to complete.

EVERY DAY IS EARTH DAY

REFERENCE:
The ecological facts are from:
50 Simple Things You Can Do To Save The Earth. The Earth Works Group,
Berkeley, California, 1989.

Necessary Knowledge: Basic fifth grade math ability.

Cooperative Collaboration: Students will share and
discuss environmental issues.

Grand Finale:
- The students could be given a similar work sheet to
  complete individually after the cooperative activity.
- The students will receive a grade on the work sheet.

Next time I plan to _____

_____

EVERY DAY IS EARTH DAY

PROBLEM CARD

The environment is being threatened by acid rain, hazardous waste, garbage, and pollution. It is the task of the cooperative group, using environmental information, to begin its own battle with the elements endangering the planet earth. Below are several facts the group should use to solve problems dealing with the environment. Familiarize the group with this information.

FACTS

- 99.5 percent of all the fresh water is in ice caps and glaciers.
- Americans receive 2 million tons of junk mail every year.
- At the rate we're generating garbage, we need 500 new dumps every year.
- Washing machines use 32 to 59 gallons of water for each cycle.
- You use 5 gallons of water if you leave the water running while you brush your teeth.
- A styrofoam cup will be here in 500 years. It is not biodegradable.
- In 1987, on the Texas beaches the following was collected: 31,773 plastic cups, 30,295 plastic bottles, 15,631 plastic six-pack rings, 28,540 plastic lids, and 1,914 disposable diapers.
- Ten years ago there were 1,500,000 elephants in Africa. Now due to ivory hunters, there are only 750,000.
- In your lifetime you will create 600 times your adult weight in garbage.
- The energy saved from one recycled aluminum can will operate a television for three hours.

EVERY DAY IS EARTH DAY

ROLE-PLAYING CARD

The Runner: If no one in the group can answer a particular question, raise your hand and ask the teacher for help.

The Recorder: You write the group's answers on the student work sheet.

The Checker: Your role is to check the work sheet for accuracy and to make certain all group members could answer the questions on their own.

The Encourager: Your job is to involve all group members in the completion of the work sheet. If someone shares a good idea, tell him/her he/she is very helpful to the group. If someone is not participating, find ways to involve him/her in the activity.

EVERY DAY IS EARTH DAY

HELPFUL HINTS

Definition:

1. Environment - all conditions that affect an organism
2. Biodegradable - describes an object that will decompose
3. Recycle - to use again
4. Decompose - to rot
5. Disposable - describes an object that can be thrown away
6. Landfill - a place for disposing of garbage by burying it in the ground
7. Junk Mail - mail received that is advertising something

Remember...

When determining a percent, remember that the whole is equal to 100 percent.

EVERY DAY IS EARTH DAY

Student Work Sheet

List the students' names by the role they selected.

Runner _____

Recorder _____

Checker _____

Encourager _____

Using the ten facts on the problem card, solve these environmental problems:

1. If your mother washes six loads of clothes per week, how much water does she use? Remember that washers have two cycles per load, wash and rinse. _____

2. What percent of fresh water comes from somewhere besides ice caps and glaciers? _____

3. How many dumps will we have in the next 10 years? _____

4. A styrofoam cup thrown away in 1991 will still be here in _____ (what year).

5. If California, Florida, and North Carolina collected as many plastic cups as Texas, how many plastic cups would these three states have all together? _____

6. If everyone in the cooperative group left the water running this morning when they brushed their teeth, how much water did the group use?

   _____

© 1991 by Incentive Publications, Inc., Nashville, TN

Every Day is Earth Day

7. How many elephants have been killed in the last ten years?

   _____

8. Every member of the cooperative group should determine how much garbage he/she creates in his/her lifetime using his/her present weight. Write down the total garbage created by the group in its lifetime.

   _____

9. List below the names of television shows that add up to three hours of viewing.

   _____

   _____

   _____

10. What is the total amount of junk mail the group will receive this year?

   _____

Discussion Question

As a group list five things you could do to help the environment.

1. _____

2. _____

3. _____

4. _____

5. _____

Every Day is Earth Day
Follow-up Activity

10 ENVIRONMENTAL FACTS

- The average American uses 7 trees in one year.
- In 6 months a leaky toilet wastes 4,500 gallons of water.
- 50 percent of trash is recyclable.
- Disposable diapers take 500 years to decompose in a landfill.
- On the beaches of America, 2 million pounds of trash were picked up in 3 hours.
- About 40 percent of all battery sales occur during Christmas.
- Washing dishes with the water running uses 30 gallons of water.
- To make one pat of butter (one small serving), it takes 100 gallons of water.
- About 44 percent of all junk mail is never opened.
- Dog and cat flea collars contain dangerous pesticides.

Using the ten facts above, answer the following questions:

1. If there were 25 students in the class, how many trees would the class use in one year? _____

2. What percent of trash cannot be recycled? _____

3. If there are 100 million dogs in the world and each dog wore two collars a year, how many flea collars would have to be disposed of?

   _____

4. What percent of junk mail is opened? _____

5. In a year, how much water is wasted by a leaky toilet? _____

6. If a stick of butter has 10 pats in it, how much water was used to make the stick? _____

7. If you washed dishes three times a day and you left the water running, how much water did you use? _____

8. What percentage of batteries is sold at times other than Christmas?_____

9. How much trash could be picked up at the beach in 24 hours?

   _____

10. Name two things you could do to help the environment.

    _____

    _____

Big Bob's

SUBJECT AREA: Mathematics

GRADE LEVEL: 5-8

SKILL: Students will place a large order from a mock restaurant.

OBJECTIVE:
- The students will place an order for 25 people at a mock McDonald's®.
- The students will be required to calculate a 10 percent discount on the order.

MATERIALS:
- "Big Bob's" problem card
- "Big Bob's" role-play card
- "Big Bob's" menu card
- "Big Bob's" helpful hints sheet
- "Big Bob's" work sheet
- Group processing work sheet
- Calculator (optional)
- Pencil
- Paper

SUGGESTION FOR POSITIVE INTERDEPENDENCE:
The students will be assigned roles during the problem-solving cooperative activity.

BIG BOB'S

SUGGESTIONS FOR ACCOUNTABILITY:
- *Group:* A group processing form will be given to the group at the end of the activity. The students will also receive a grade on the "Big Bob's" work sheet.
- *Individual:* The individual must complete his/her specific responsibility during the lesson.

Necessary Knowledge:
- The students should have basic math skills consistent with an average fifth grade student.
- The students should have a basic understanding of percentage-type problems.

Cooperative Collaboration: Students must read the cards included in the problem-solving boxes together. The group is then assigned specific roles to perform.

Grand Finale:
- The students will complete a group processing form after completing the activity.
- The cooperative group will receive a grade on the problem-solving activity.
- An actual field trip could be planned to a local fast food restaurant.

Next time I plan to _____

_____

Big Bob's

Twenty-five friends are coming to Mary's little sister's birthday party. Mary's sister is hoping for a party at Big Bob's. Mary's parents have put her in charge of all the details, and they have given her $90.

The party representative stated that if the entire bill is over $50, they give a 10 percent discount. The following questions must be answered in order to have a successful party.

- What will Mary serve the twenty-five kids at the party?
- Would it be wise to order a special kid's meal for everybody?
- What is the total bill for the party?
- How much of the $90 will be left?
- How much did Mary save due to the discount?
- If the tax rate is 7.75 percent, what is the tax on the total bill?

ROLE-PLAYING CARD

Assign the following roles to the group:

Mary: The party planner. She must decide what she will order for the party.	**Big Bob's Manager:** He/she must figure the 10 percent discount.
Big Bob's Counter Worker: He/she must write down the order.	**Mary's mother or father:** Places the order and makes certain Big Bob's gives the correct discount and returns the correct amount of change.

BIG BOB'S

MENU

Hamburger .... .90
Cheeseburger 1.00
Fish Sandwich...1.15
1/4 lb. 1.35
1/4 lb. w/cheese...1.45
Big Bob 1.35
6 Piece Chicken Tenders 1.35
12 Piece Chicken Tenders................................1.89
Kid's Meals (hamburger, small fries, small soft drink, prize)..................2.25
Regular Fries...57
Large Fries 75
Peach/Apricot Pies 50
Cookies 45
Sundaes 65
Cones 35
Milk..45
Regular Drink 65
Large Drink..75

BIG BOB'S

HELPFUL HINTS

Hint 1
    1. How to find a percentage of a number:
        Multiply the total amount times the percent.
        Example: Total amount $72.00 x .10 (10%) = 7.20

    2. How to find the total discounted bill:
        Example: $72.00 - 7.20 = $64.80

Hint 2
    1. How to calculate the sales tax.
        Multiply the total amount times 7.75%
        Example: total discounted amount = $64.80 x .0775 (7.75%) = $5.02

    2. How to arrive at the total bill
        Add $64.80 + 5.02 = $69.82

Work Space

Names _____

Big Bob's

1. List the name of each group member and his/her role.

   Mary _____

   Big Bob's Manager _____

   Big Bob's Counter Worker _____

   Parent _____

2. Did the group decide to order kid's meals for everybody? _____

   Why or why not? _____

3. What will be served at the party? _____

   _____

   _____

4. Fill in the order blank below:

Quantity	Item	Price each	Total price

5. What is the total bill (without the discount or taxes)? _____

6. What is the discount Mary received? _____

7. What were the taxes on the order? _____

8. What is the total bill including taxes and the discount? _____

Names _____

CDs and You

SUBJECT AREA: Mathematics

GRADE LEVEL: 5-8

SKILL: The students will evaluate the pros and cons of joining a mail order CD club.

OBJECTIVES:
- The students will decide cooperatively on eight specific CDs.
- The students will add decimal numbers.

MATERIALS:
- "CDs and You" problem card
- "CDs and You" role-playing card
- "CDs and You" selection sheet (or an actual CD club advertisement)
- "CDs and You" student work sheet
- "CDs and You" group processing sheet
- Calculator (optional)

SUGGESTION FOR POSITIVE INTERDEPENDENCE:
The students will have to function as one unit when selecting the eight CDs.

CDs and You

SUGGESTIONS FOR ACCOUNTABILITY:
- *Group:* Each student must agree on the answers on the work sheet.
- *Individual:* Each student will have a portion of the student work sheet to complete.

Necessary Knowledge: The ability to add decimal numbers.

Cooperative Collaboration: Most students will vary in musical tastes, so it will be an exercise in cooperation to decide on the selection of CDs.

Grand Finale: A student group processing activity should be done at the close of this activity.

Teacher's Note: An actual advertisement from a CD club would be great to use with the students. If that is not possible, a CD selection sheet is provided.

Next time I plan to _____

CDs and You

8 CDs for Only 1 Penny

Order any 8 CDs for 1 penny (plus shipping and handling with membership details below).

Here is how to accept this opportunity.

1. Just mail the order blank with a check or money order for $1.86 (that is shipping and handling plus 1 penny).
2. Agree to buy 8 more selections in the next 2 years at regular club prices ($12.98 to $15.98); then you can cancel your membership at any time.
3. Every month we will send you a listing of CDs. The monthly selection will be sent to you *automatically* if you do nothing. If you prefer an alternate selection or none at all, just mail the response card back indicating your selection or rejection.
4. **Trial membership -** If you are not satisfied, you can return the 8 CDs within 10 days and there is no further obligation.
5. **Extra Bonus Offer -** You can take one additional CD right now at $7.95; then you are entitled to take an extra CD as a bonus FREE. You'll receive the discounted CD and the bonus CD, plus the 8 FREE selections!

The group must decide the following:

- Will the group take advantage of the extra bonus offer?
- What CDs does the group want to order?
- How much will joining the CD club cost over the two-year period?
- What is the average cost of the free CDs and the regular priced CDs?

CDs AND YOU

ROLE-PLAYING CARDS

Character 1: Working cooperatively with the group, decide on 8 CDs the group would like to order. Fill in the portion of the order blank that asks for the CD names. Also, decide which group member's name will be used on the CD membership card.

Character 2: Working cooperatively with the group, decide if it is best to take advantage of the extra bonus offer. If the group decides to choose the two additional CDs, fill in the portion of the order blank that asks for two additional CD names.

Character 3: Decide how much it will cost the group to buy 8 more CDs over the next two years. Estimate that the average cost of the the CDs will be $14.50 each.

Character 4: Determine how much it will cost the group to receive the eight free CDs, the bonus CDs, and the eight additional CDs that must be purchased over the next two years. (Use the average price of $14.50 for the eight additional CDs).

CDs and You

CD Selection Card

Choose CDs from the list below:

Bobby Brown - *Dance…Ya Know It*
Paula Abdul - *Forever Your Girl*
Young M.C. - *Stone Cold Rhymin'*
Aerosmith - *Pump*
Tommy Page - *Painting In My Mind*
Elton John - *Greatest Hits*
Tom Petty - *Full Moon Forever*
Bruce Hornsby - *A Night On The Town*
Janet Jackson - *Rhythm Nation 1814*
B-52's - *Cosmic Thing*
Dave Grusin - *Migration*
The Rave-Ups - *Chance*
Chunky A - *Large And In Charge*
Moody Blues - *Greatest Hits*
Jimi Hendrix - *Electric Ladyland*
Pat Benatar - *Best Shots*
Stevie Wonder - *20 Great Love Songs*
Phil Collins - *12 Inches*
The Police - *The Singles*
Whitesnake - *Slip Of The Tongue*
Jive Presents: *Yo! MTV Raps*
Bon Jovi - *New Jersey*
Whitney Houston - *Whitney*
M.C. Hammer - *Please Hammer Don't Hurt 'Em*
Van Halen - *OU812*
Olivia Newton John - *Warm And Tender*
Tracy Chapman - *Crossroad*
Elvis Presley - *18 Number One Hits*
Beethoven - *Symphony No. 9*
Prince - *Batman*
Taylor Dane - *Can't Fight Fate*
Tina Turner - *Foreign Affair*
Kenny G and others - *Happy Anniversary Charlie Brown*
Cher - *Heart of Stone*
Motley Crue - *Dr. Feelgood*
The Beach Boys - *Made In The USA*
Clint Black - *Killin' Time*

CDs and You

Student Work Sheet

Write the name of each member of the group and the role each represents.

Character 1 _____

Character 2 _____

Character 3 _____

Character 4 _____

Fill in the order blank for the CD club membership.

Order Blank

Please accept my application for membership in the CD club. I'm enclosing a check or money order for $1.86. I agree to buy 8 more CDs in the next two years at regular prices, and I understand that I can cancel my membership at any time after doing so. Send me these 8 CDs for 1 penny.

Write your selections below:

1. _____

2. _____

3. _____

4. _____

5. _____

6. _____

7. _____

8. _____

Extra Bonus Offer

Also, send me one more CD now, for which I am enclosing an additional $7.95, and I'm entitled to this extra CD FREE!

1. _____

2. _____

My main musical interest is (circle one):

Hard Rock	Soft Rock	Rap	Oldies	Classical
Heavy Metal	Soul Music	Easy Listening	Country	Jazz

❑ Mr.
❑ Mrs.
❑ Miss _____
     Print   First Name   Initial   Last Name

Address _____

City_____ State _____ Zip _____

Do you have a credit card? Yes ❑   No ❑

Number & Expiration _____

CDs and You

Questions

1. How much will it cost the group to receive 8 more CDs over the next two years if the average cost of the CDs is $14.50? _____

2. What is the total cost of the 2 year commitment to the CD club?

   _____

   (Be sure to include the initial charge, the bonus offer, and the 8 additional CDs that must be purchased.)

3. Decide as a group if joining the club is a good idea. Write below if the group will join and tell why or why not.

   _____

   _____

   _____

© 1991 by Incentive Publications, Inc., Nashville, TN

Names _____

CDs and You

Was it easy for the group to decide on 8 CDs to order?
Yes ❑ No ❑

If there was a disagreement, how did the group decide on what to order?

_____

_____

List the group members' names who are very pleased with all the selections.

_____

List the group members' names who are somewhat satisfied with the selections the group chose. _____

List the group members' names who are unhappy with the selections the group chose. _____

_____

_____

The best cooperative thing we did was _____

_____

_____

Next time we need to improve by _____

Names _____

CDs AND You

Name _____ **My job was ...**

_____

_____

_____

_____

_____

Circle the answer your group agrees with for the following questions.

1. Everyone in our group helped with the assignment.

    Yes   No

2. We made certain everyone understood the assignment.

    Yes   No

3. We did a good job listening to everyone's ideas.

    Yes   No

4. Today the best cooperative thing we did was _____

_____

_____

_____

5. Next time we need to improve by _____

_____

_____

_____

EVERY WHICH WAY BUT "LOSE"

SUBJECT AREA: Any subject

GRADE LEVEL: 4-9

OBJECTIVES: Using a game format, students will review material learned in the cooperative group.

MATERIALS:
- "Cooperative Game Directions" sheet
- An "Every Which Way But 'Lose'" game board. This can be used effectively as an overhead.
- Markers for each team (small pieces of paper cut in different shapes work well on the overhead)

SUGGESTION FOR POSITIVE INTERDEPENDENCE:
The cooperative teams play against each other. The questions should rotate throughout the entire group. Winning depends on *all group members* knowing the material.

SUGGESTIONS FOR ACCOUNTABILITY:
- *Group:* The groups should make certain all students know the assigned material.
- *Individual:* The individual student must be prepared to answer any questions asked.

Necessary Knowledge: The students must have completed a cooperative activity where a certain body of material was taught.

Cooperative Collaboration: The team must play the game as one unit.

Grand Finale: The group winners could receive a reward.

Next time I plan to _____

_____

EVERY WHICH WAY BUT "LOSE"

Cooperative Game Directions

1. Each cooperative team places a marker on start.

2. A die is rolled to determine the value of spaces a particular question is worth.

3. Someone asks a question. If answered correctly, the team or the player can move the amount of spaces on the die. Moves can be taken in any direction except diagonally.

4. If the move ends on an arrow, the first space in the next move **must** follow the direction of the arrow. If the move ends on a square, the next move can go in any direction.

5. The object of the game is to be the first to reach home. This must be accomplished by using up all the spaces on the die.

EVERY WHICH WAY BUT "LOSE"

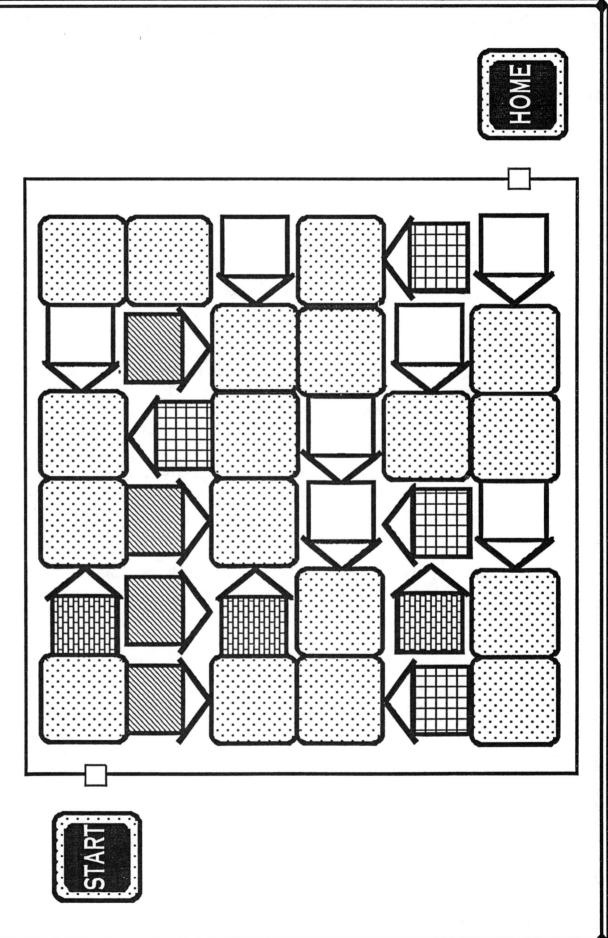

ANSWERS

THE THINKING "T"

TANGRAM I WORK SHEET

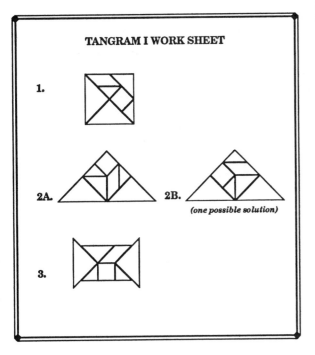

1.

2A.   2B.
(one possible solution)

3.

YEAH FOR YARN!

QUIZ

Name the geometric figure that has:

1. Ten sides ___Decagon___

2. Eight sides ___Octagon___

3. Six sides ___Hexagon___

4. Three sides ___Triangle___

5. Nine sides ___Nonagon___

6. Seven sides ___Heptagon___

7. Five sides ___Pentagon___

8. Four congruent sides with the opposite sides parallel ___Rhombus___

9. Four sides with the opposite sides congruent and parallel ___Parallelogram___

10. Three congruent sides ___Equilateral Triangle___

PRIME TIME

1. Build as many rectangles as possible using two to twelve cubes, and record your results on this chart.

Number of Blocks	Different Widths	Number of Widths
Example: 2	(1, 2) (2,1)	2
3	(1, 3), (3,1)	2
4	(1, 4), (4,1), (2, 2)	3
5	(1, 5), (5, 1)	2
6	(1, 6) (6,1), (2, 3), (3, 2)	4
7	(1, 7), (7, 1)	2
8	(1, 8), (8,1), (2, 4), (4, 2)	4
9	(1, 9), (9, 1), (3, 3)	3
10	(1, 10), (10,1), (2, 5), (5, 2)	4
11	(1, 11), (11,1)	2
12	(1,12), (12, 1), (2, 6), (6, 2), (3, 4), (4, 3)	6

2. What do you notice about the relationship of the number of blocks to the different widths?

   ___The different widths tell the factors.___

3. What are some common factors of 2 and 4? ___1 & 2___
   • 3 and 9? ___1 & 3___
   • 6 and 12? ___1, 2, 3, & 6___

4. What is the greatest common factor of 3 and 12? ___3___
   • 2 and 6? ___2___
   • 8 and 12? ___4___
   • 7 and 3? ___1___

5. Look on your chart and circle the numbers that have exactly two widths. These numbers are called prime numbers. What can you tell about the relationship between the blocks that are prime numbers and the number of widths? ___Prime numbers have only two factors.___

6. Look on your chart at the numbers that aren't circled. These are called composite numbers. What can you tell about the relationship between composite numbers and the number of widths? ___Composite numbers have more than two factors.___

PRIME TIME

THE SIEVE OF ERATOSTHENES

STEP 1: Cross off 1.

STEP 2: Circle 2, and using colored pencils, shade in every number that is evenly divisible by 2.

STEP 3: Circle 3 and shade in every number that is evenly divisible by 3.

STEP 4: Circle 5 and shade in every number that is evenly divisible by 5.

STEP 5: Circle 7 and shade in every number that is evenly divisible by 7.

X	②	③	4	⑤	6	⑦	8	9	10
11	12	13	14	15	16	17	18	19	20
21	22	23	24	25	26	27	28	29	30
31	32	33	34	35	36	37	38	39	40
41	42	43	44	45	46	47	48	49	50
51	52	53	54	55	56	57	58	59	60
61	62	63	64	65	66	67	68	69	70
71	72	73	74	75	76	77	78	79	80
81	82	83	84	85	86	87	88	89	90
91	92	93	94	95	96	97	98	99	100

Note to teacher:
Prime numbers plain type.
Composite numbers underlined.

ANSWERS

COOPERATIVE SOUP

Double and rewrite the following recipe:

Original Ingredients	Doubled Ingredients
1 c. frozen green beans	2 c. frozen green beans
1 clove of garlic	2 cloves of garlic
28 oz. of tomatoes	56 oz. (3 1/2 lbs) can of tomatoes
6 oz. tomato paste	12 oz. tomato paste
2 t. sugar	4 t. sugar
3 T. oil	6 T. oil

Write the word that each abbreviation represents.

1). c. __cup__   5). T. __tablespoon__

2). t. __teaspoon__   6). oz. __ounce__

3). lb. __pound__   7). pt. __pint__

4). qt. __quart__   8). gal. __gallon__

In each blank write teaspoon(s), cup(s), quarts(s), or gallon(s).

1. A typical dosage of cough syrup for a child is 2 ___teaspoons___ .

2. A glass of orange juice is 1 ___cup___ .

3. A recipe calls for 1 ___teaspoon___ of salt.

4. The cookie recipe calls for 2 ___cups___ of sugar.

5. The punch recipe calls for 2 ___qts. or gal.___ of water.

Complete.

1). 1 c. __8__ oz.   4). 2 gal. __8__ qt.   7). 6 c. __3__ pt.

2). 1 T. __3__ t.   5). 3 c. __24__ oz.   8). 1 lb. __16__ oz.

3). 3 qt. __6__ pt.   6). 16 oz. __1__ lb.   9). 2 c. __16__ oz.

Enrichment
If Cooperative Soup yields 1 gallon of soup and there are 24 students in the class,
how many ounces of soup will each student receive? _____

__5 1/3 ounce servings.   1 gal = 128 fl oz.   128 ÷ 24 = 5 1/3__

43

CONFUSED ABOUT CONVEX?

Determining the sum of the measures of the angles of convex polygons:

1. Build a four-sided polygon on the geoboard. Put a rubber band over the peg at any vertex and stretch it to the peg at an opposite vertex. A line connecting two vertices that are not next to each other is called a diagonal. Can you make another diagonal starting at the same vertex? _____

2. Fill in the following chart by building the polygons and finding the number of diagonals that can be drawn from each vertex. When you finish, leave the octagon and its diagonals on your board.

Polygon	Number Of Sides	Number Of Diagonals From One Vertex
Triangle	3	0
Quadrilateral	4	1
Pentagon	5	2
Hexagon	6	3
Octagon	8	5

• What is the relationship between the numbers of diagonals from one vertex and the number of sides in a polygon? _____

___there is a difference of 3___   (n-3)

• How many diagonals are in a 10-sided polygon? __7__
• How many diagonals are in a 50-sided polygon? __47__

3. What shapes are made inside the octagon on your geoboard? _____

___Triangles___

• How many triangles are inside this polygon? __6__

45

CONFUSED ABOUT CONVEX?

Fill in the following chart by building the polygons and marking the diagonals to determine the number of triangles on your geoboard.

Polygon	Number Of Sides	Number Of Triangles
Triangle	3	1
Quadrilateral	4	2
Pentagon	5	3
Hexagon	6	4
Octagon	8	6

• What is the relationship between the number of triangles and the number of sides? ___there is a difference of 2___   (n-2)
• How many triangles are in a 10-sided polygon? __8__
• How many triangles are in a 50-sided polygon? __48__

4. Are all the angles of the octagon part of a triangle? __yes__
What is the sum of the angles of a triangle? __180°__
How many triangles are in an octagon? __6__
So, what is the the sum of the angles of an octagon?
___(n-2) x 180°___   6 x 180° = 1080°

Now fill in the following chart.

Polygon	(n-2) Number Of Triangles	(n-2) x 180° Sum Of All The Angles
Triangle	1	(3-2) x 180° = 180°
Quadrilateral	2	(4-2) x 180° = 360°
Pentagon	3	(5-2) x 180° = 540°
Hexagon	4	(6-2) x 180° = 720°
Octagon	6	(8-2) x 180° = 1080°

46

ANSWERS

DON'T CATCH COMMA FEVER!

When it comes to commas, students often catch "comma fever." This is a very common disease that affects middle school students. It is deadly to a sentence. Please avoid this dreaded disease. It will plague you to failure. The first symptom of this dangerous fever could be a failing grade on a language arts assignment. If it is not cured immediately, a student's language arts report card grade drops to a dangerous level. The worst part of the disease is that parents may begin to request that their child spend one hour a night studying language arts. (This hour occurs when a favorite television show is on.) Please be careful and avoid this disease. Always have a reason to place a comma!

With your cooperative group member, place commas correctly in each sentence. Write the rule you used in your decision to place the comma. A score of 90 percent will ensure that the comma disease has not invaded your mind...yet!

1. I live in Nashville, Tennessee.
Rule __5__

2. She was born on August 29, 1955, and now she lives in Columbus, Ohio.
Rule __4__
Rule __2__
Rule __5__

3. Joe Smith, the mailman, lives two blocks away.
Rule __3__

4. June, July, August, and September are the summer months.
Rule __1__

5. What did you tell the doctor, Jane?
Rule __3__

6. Please forward all my mail to 331 Anywhere Drive, Nashville, Tennessee.
Rule __5__

7. John went to school in Dallas, Texas, and Bill went to school in Boise, Idaho.
Rule __5__
Rule __2__
Rule __5__

8. Florida, a favorite vacation spot, is a beautiful state.
Rule __3__

9. Lincoln was shot on April 14, 1865, in Washington, D.C.
Rule __4__
Rule __5__

58

DON'T CATCH COMMA FEVER!

10. She was going to call her mother, but she forgot.
Rule __2__

11. Karen was supposed to buy butter, cheese, milk, and ice cream.
Rule __1__

12. I went to Dr. Smith, a famous brain surgeon, to get relief from comma fever.
Rule __3__

13. Bill, Mary, Joe, Helen, and I went to the football game.
Rule __1__

14. Mary, do you have a dime?
Rule __3__

15. My mother lives in San Diego, California.
Rule __5__

In the following letter, place commas correctly.

> 331 Anywhere
> Nashville, Tennessee 11111
> July 4, 1990
>
> Dear Sam,
>
> I just can't believe it! Dr. Art, a famous physician, said I have comma fever. My first hint of the disease came when I did not bother learning my rules for commas. Soon I, an "A" student, was putting commas everywhere! Commas, periods, semicolons, and exclamation marks were everywhere on my paper. My grades declined in language arts. As my fever went up, my grades went down. My grades were 80, 77, 66, 50, and 42. I got a 32, and my mother grounded me. Please come by and see me. Sam, bring my language arts book, my reading book, and my spelling book. Dr. Art, my physician, said studying my lessons is the only cure.
>
> Your feverish friend,
>
> Fred

59

PARADE OF PLANETS

Step 1: Mercury, Venus, Earth, Mars, Jupiter, Saturn, Uranus, Neptune, and Pluto are planets in our solar system. First, cooperatively decide which group members will research which planets. For each planet the following facts must be found:
1. How far is the planet from the sun?
2. What is the planet's diameter? (Remember, the diameter is the distance all the way across the planet.)
3. What color does the planet appear to be, or what unusual characteristics does it have?

When the research has been completed, fill in the following fact sheet.

Planet Name ___Mercury___
Distance from the sun _36,000,000 miles_
Color or characteristics __gray__
___It is full of craters & cracks___
Diameter _3,010 miles_

Planet Name ___Venus___
Distance from the sun _67,200,000 miles_
Color or characteristics __bright silver__
___Silvering clouds___
Diameter __7,620 miles__

Planet Name ___Earth___
Distance from the sun _93,000,000 miles_
Color or characteristics __blue__

Diameter __7,900 miles__

Planet Name ___Mars___
Distance from the sun _142,000,000 miles_
Color or characteristics __red__

Diameter __4,220 miles__

Planet Name ___Jupiter___
Distance from the sun _484,000,000 miles_
Color or characteristics __whitish yellow__

Diameter __88,800 miles__

Planet Name ___Saturn___
Distance from the sun _886,000,000 miles_
Color or characteristics
___yellow___
Diameter __74,000 miles__

Planet Name ___Uranus___
Distance from the sun _1,780,000,000 miles_
Color or characteristics
___Spins on its side___
Diameter __29,500 miles__

Planet Name ___Neptune___
Distance from the sun _2,800,000,000 miles_
Color or characteristics
___Wobbles when it orbits___
Diameter __27,200 miles__

Planet Name ___Pluto___
Distance from the sun _3,660,000,000 miles_
Color or characteristics
___Cold & very dark___
Diameter __1,900 miles__

78

WHAT CAUSES THE SEASONS?

Student Instruction Sheet

1. Shine a flashlight as shown in diagram 1.

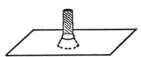

Diagram 1

What kind of area is covered by the light as it shines on the paper? _____
Trace this area on the paper. Now shine your flashlight on the same sheet of paper as shown in diagram 2.

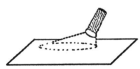

Diagram 2

Trace the area. What do you notice about the different areas? _____
___The area when the light is direct is a smaller area.___
In which area, direct or slanted, do you think the temperature would be
greater? _____Direct_____

2. Divide your cooperative learning team into two groups with two members in each group. Each group will need a flashlight, thermometer, a piece of black construction paper, and a chart for graphing its results.

81

155

ANSWERS

WHAT CAUSES THE SEASONS?

4. Tell what you discovered about the difference in the temperature of the light when it is direct and when it is slanted.

When the light is direct, the temperature is hotter.

_____
_____
_____

5. Use a globe and a flashlight to explain how the slant of the sun's rays causes the seasons.

6. As a group decide how you think life as we know it would be changed if the earth did not tilt on its axis. Tell what you think life would be like at the equator, in the northern hemisphere, southern hemisphere, and at the north and south poles.

_____
_____

Answers will vary.

_____
_____
_____

83

MUSIC MADNESS

Character 1

Concerts	Ticket Cost
Answers will vary	Answers will vary

Total parking costs _____
Total cost _____
(Did you have any money left? How much?) _____

Character 2

How many songs will the Temptations sing?	13
How many songs will the Four Tops sing?	24
Which group will sing the most songs?	The Four Tops
How many more songs?	11

Example for how to divide mixed numbers:

$$2\tfrac{1}{3} + 1\tfrac{1}{3} =$$
$$\tfrac{7}{3} + \tfrac{4}{3} =$$
$$\tfrac{7}{3} \times \tfrac{4}{4} = \tfrac{11}{3} = 1\tfrac{1}{3}$$

112

MUSIC MADNESS

Character 3

How much do you earn per week?	76.00
How much will you pay in taxes?	7.60
Subtract these numbers (This is your take-home pay.)	68.40
How much money do you have to spend?	_____

List ticket prices

Elton John	18.50
Aerosmith	19.50
Don Henley	19.50
Janet Jackson	22.00
Eric Clapton	22.00
New Kids on the Block	24.00
Total costs	125.50

How long would you have to work to buy one reserved seat ticket to each concert?	2 weeks
How long would you have to work to buy two reserved seat tickets?	4 weeks

Character 4

What is the average price of a general admission ticket? about 17.83
What would be the average price of ten general admission tickets? 178.30
Should you buy the Music Club Card or individual tickets?
Music Club Card
How much money would you save? 53.30

113

McSOVIET

STUDENT WORK SHEET

1. List the name of each group member and the character he/she was assigned.
   Character 1 _____
   Character 2 _____
   Character 3 _____
   Character 4 _____

2. What is the average Soviet wage for one day? 18 rubles

3. What percentage of this wage does a meal at McDonald's® cost? 31%

4. Does the average worker make enough in one day to feed a family of four? _____ Explain your answer, and list what was purchased for the family. _____
_____

5. How many times would the restaurant have to be filled in order to serve the record crowd on opening day? 40

118

156

ANSWERS

EVERY DAY IS EARTH DAY

Student Work Sheet

List the students' names by the role they selected.

Runner _____

Recorder _____

Checker _____

Encourager _____

Using the ten facts on the problem card, solve these environmental problems:

1. If your mother washes six loads of clothes per week, how much water does she use? Remember that washers have two cycles per load, wash and rinse. __384-708 gal.__

2. What percent of fresh water comes from somewhere besides ice caps and glaciers? ___.5%___

3. How many dumps will we have in the next 10 years? ___5,000___

4. A styrofoam cup thrown away in 1991 will still be here in ___2,491___ (what year).

5. If California, Florida, and North Carolina collected as many plastic cups as Texas, how many plastic cups would these three states have all together? ___95,319___

6. If everyone in the cooperative group left the water running this morning when they brushed their teeth, how much water did the group use?

_____

132

EVERY DAY IS EARTH DAY

7. How many elephants have been killed in the last ten years? ___750,000___

8. Every member of the cooperative group should determine how much garbage he/she creates in his/her lifetime using his/her present weight. Write down the total garbage created by the group in its lifetime.

_____

9. List below the names of television shows that add up to three hours of viewing.

_____

_____

_____

10. What is the total amount of junk mail the group will receive this year?

_____

Discussion Question

As a group list five things you could do to help the environment.

1. _____

2. _____

3. _____

4. _____

5. _____

133

EVERY DAY IS EARTH DAY
FOLLOW-UP ACTIVITY

10 ENVIRONMENTAL FACTS

- The average American uses 7 trees in one year.
- In 6 months a leaky toilet wastes 4,500 gallons of water.
- 50 percent of trash is recyclable.
- Disposable diapers take 500 years to decompose in a landfill.
- On the beaches of America, 2 million pounds of trash were picked up in 3 hours.
- About 40 percent of all battery sales occur during Christmas.
- Washing dishes with the water running uses 30 gallons of water.
- To make one pat of butter (one small serving), it takes 100 gallons of water.
- About 44 percent of all junk mail is never opened.
- Dog and cat flea collars contain dangerous pesticides.

Using the ten facts above, answer the following questions:

1. If there were 25 students in the class, how many trees would the class use in one year? ___175___

2. What percent of trash cannot be recycled? ___50%___

3. If there are 100 million dogs in the world and each dog wore two collars a year, how many flea collars would have to be disposed of? ___200 million___

4. What percent of junk mail is opened? ___56%___

5. In a year, how much water is wasted by a leaky toilet? ___9,000 gallons___

6. If a stick of butter has 10 pats in it, how much water was used to make the stick? ___1,000 gallons___

7. If you washed dishes three times a day and you left the water running, how much water did you use? ___90 gallons___

8. What percentage of batteries is sold at times other than Christmas? _60%_

9. How much trash could be picked up at the beach in 24 hours? ___16 million pounds___

10. Name two things you could do to help the environment. ___Answers will vary.___

134

CDs AND YOU

Student Work Sheet

Questions

1. How much will it cost the group to receive 8 more CDs over the next two years if the average cost of the CDs is $14.50? ___$116.00___

2. What is the total cost of the 2 year commitment to the CD club? ___$125.81___

(Be sure to include the initial charge, the bonus offer, and the 8 additional CDs that must be purchased.)

3. Decide as a group if joining the club is a good idea. Write below if the group will join and tell why or why not.

_____

_____

_____

147

157

REFERENCES

Bell, N., (1981). *The book of where or how to be naturally geographic.* Boston, Little, Brown, and Company.

Carin A., & Sund, R., (1975) *Teaching science through discovery.* Columbus, Charles E. Merrill.

Jobb, J. (1977). *The night sky book. An everyday guide to every night.* Boston, Little, Brown, and Company.

Johnson, D., Johnson, R. & Holubec, E. (1988). *Advanced cooperative learning.* Minnesota, Interaction Book Company.

Johnson, D. & Johnson, R. (1989 December - January) Social skills for successful group work. *Educational Leadership*, pp. 20-33.

Kagan, S. (1989). *Cooperative learning resources for teachers.* California, Resources for Teachers.

Rees, Rebecca D. (1990, April). Station Break: A mathematics games book using cooperative learning and role playing. *Arithmetic Teacher 37,* 8-12.

Shearer, P. (1990, March). Relating critical thinking skills to math classes. Presented at the Southeastern Regional Conference of the National Teachers of Mathematics, Chattanooga, TN.

Wilmot, B., (1985). Creative problem solving and red yarn. *Arithmetic Teacher, 33,* 3-5.

NOTES: